MICHIGAN

MYTHS & LEGENDS

MICHIGAN

MYTHS & LEGENDS

THE TRUE STORIES BEHIND HISTORY'S MYSTERIES

SECOND EDITION

SALLY BARBER

Globe
Pequot

Guilford, Connecticut

Globe
Pequot

An imprint of The Rowman & Littlefield Publishing Group, Inc.
4501 Forbes Blvd., Ste. 200
Lanham, MD 20706
www.rowman.com

Distributed by NATIONAL BOOK NETWORK

Copyright © 2020 by The Rowman & Littlefield Publishing Group, Inc.

Map by Daniel Lloyd

British Library Cataloguing in Publication Information available

Library of Congress Cataloging-in-Publication Data available

ISBN 978-1-4930-4008-7 (paper : alk. paper)
ISBN 978-1-4930-4009-4 (electronic)

∞™ The paper used in this publication meets the minimum requirements of American National Standard for Information Sciences—Permanence of Paper for Printed Library Materials, ANSI/NISO Z39.48-1992

To my family

CONTENTS

INTRODUCTION

Michigan is an amazing state. From the Mitten's towering coastal dunes to Detroit's historic Woodward Avenue to the wilds of the Keweenaw Peninsula, Michigan embodies an unparalleled natural majesty and a human spirit characterized by industriousness, innovation, and a sense of justice. Just how deep these threads run was a surprise to this author, who has written about the state for more than twenty years. As you delve into the pages of *Michigan Myths and Legends,* you will be reminded of our greatness and discover a side of Michigan you never knew existed. This is the Michigan we didn't learn about in school.

You're about to examine some dark secrets, surprising legends, and a few skeletons hidden in the Michigan closet. A few facts are about to come to light, like the economy of bootlegging during Prohibition, when illegal alcohol trade ranked second only to Detroit's auto industry in revenues generated. You'll also be astonished to learn that Michigan's "Green Rush" (the lumber era), which took place during the same years as California's Gold Rush, actually exceeded the Gold Rush in revenues.

In crime as in industry, Michiganders have proven themselves to be ingenious. If you think the Batmobile is something special, you'll enjoy reading about the crime mobile the Purple Gang developed in the 1930s. Do you dream of winning the lottery? Why not join the search for the hundreds of millions of dollars' worth of smuggled gold coins believed to be lying at the bottom of Lake Michigan near Escanaba?

Is your image of rural Michigan that of picturesque red barns and freshly painted white church steeples? Look at the underside of the Mitten's history. The Wild West was tame compared with Michigan during the great lumbering era, when Roscommon was considered the wildest town in America. At the industry's peak, lumberjacks emerged from the forest by the thousands each spring to squander their money at river town "vice resorts." When fellows became intolerably rowdy, they were booted out of some establishments via chutes dropping them directly into the water—Michigan ingenuity!

While Michigan forests provided for a prosperous industry, they also spawned some of the Mitten's most intriguing legends. Inside these pages, you'll find out how the Dogman legend was born and whether Bigfoot really roams here. Equally mysterious are the sudden disappearances of Great Lakes ships and aircraft and episodes of UFO sightings. Extraterrestrial mysteries get attention, in part thanks to a surprising source—the late former President Gerald Ford. Ford's Presidential Library and Museum in Ann Arbor and Grand Rapids are considered among the best in existence. But did you know that when he was a Michigan congressman, he fought to hold UFO hearings? In chapter eight, you can read excerpts from his radio addresses on the topic gleaned from the Ford archives.

From the days of slavery to the days of Motown, Michigan has played a central role in American history. It's an intriguing fusion of heroism and subterfuge. Learn the details of union leader Jimmy Hoffa's mysterious disappearance from Detroit. Hoffa was accused of underworld dealings but also led the labor movement that provided generations of Americans with fair wages and good working conditions. Read how other men driven by greed met untimely ends. Michiganders Rose Will Monroe and Geraldine Hoff Doyle were the face of Rosie the Riveter during World War II war bond campaigns. The Rosie promotion empowered millions of women to take charge of their lives and still influences us for the better today. Even the mythical Paul Bunyan played a heroic role in the nation by providing inspiration to thousands of World War II soldiers.

As you make your way through the chapters of this book, I hope you will gain a new perspective and greater pride for the courageous and inventive Michigan citizens of our past, who, with all their human foibles made great the one and only Mitten state.

CHAPTER 1

Delta County's Treasure Island

Brutal winds often batter Poverty Island, where Karl Jessen spent the summer days of his boyhood. Playing along the isle's rocky coast, the lightkeeper's son was no doubt aware that its unforgiving landscape and surrounding treacherous waters harbored legends of vast sunken treasure.

Then one blustery summer day, from his perch along the beach Jessen watched a group of divers conduct a hunt for the chests of gold said to lie at the bottom of Lake Michigan near the Poverty Island Passage. What Jessen witnessed that day would years later trigger a diver's gold rush, drawing thousands of treasure hunters to the site.

Today, Poverty Island is uninhabited and owned by the federal government. Located twenty-seven miles southeast of the community of Escanaba within Fairbanks Township in the Upper Peninsula's Delta County, it is one of a chain of islands spanning the approach to Wisconsin's Green Bay between Wisconsin's Door Peninsula and Michigan's Garden Peninsula. The strait between the Wisconsin peninsula and the chain's major island, Washington Island, has long held the ominous name "Death's Door."

During the early days of Great Lakes maritime trade, many ships headed for the Mackinac Straits linking Lake Michigan and Lake Huron traversed the Poverty Island passage between Poverty and Gull Islands. This, too, was a highly dangerous route. Shoals caused vessels to travel close to Poverty Island's south shore, where water depths averaged a safe seventy feet.

It wasn't until 1874 that the United States Coast Guard established the first light station on Poverty Island to aid navigation through these hazardous waterways. The now abandoned sixty-foot tower and keeper's dwelling were constructed just one hundred feet from the island's south shore. Before the light existed to guide ships, both large and small vessels succumbed to the ruthless waterways. Without a natural harbor, fierce winds and waves continuously pummeled Poverty Island's rocky and desolate coastline, keeping away all but the most serious travelers.

Life for the keeper's children, like Jessen, could be monotonous and boring. A Clarke Historical Library document recounts how Poverty Island's children once got into mischief using the keeper's leftover paint to deface the station. The most serious offenders among the children were locked in a coal bin as punishment. But, the report states, every island child understood their family's serious mission and knew better than to touch the lifesaving lights.

In this bygone era lacking television and electronic games, island children must have played and replayed the legends of brave seafarers and glorious booty. Poverty Island's tales of sunken riches are almost as prolific as the tales of sunken treasure in the world's oceans, providing Mitten children of days gone by with ample material for their young imaginations. Several of these legends are detailed in Frederick Stonehouse's book, *Great Lakes Lighthouse Tales*. One enduring rumor claims that during the French and Indian War of 1754 to 1763, the British attacked a French vessel carrying treasure with which the French forces planned to purchase trade goods from Native Americans in order to secure their loyalty. To prevent the riches from falling into the wrong hands, the ship's captain chained the treasure chests together and tossed them overboard near Poverty Island.

Another tale maintains that during the War of 1812, a band of Great Lakes' pirates attacked a ship transporting military payroll. Supposedly, that ship's captain also chained together its chests of gold and flung them into the depths of Lake Michigan.

The strangest tale holds that the chest of gold believed to be hidden at the seabed near Poverty Island once belonged to the self-proclaimed "king" of nearby Beaver Island. The legend maintains that James Strang, the leader of a Mormon colony on Beaver Island, had collected the gold from his followers. In 1856, Strang was assassinated by unhappy followers, after which his box of gold mysteriously ended up on the bottomland near Poverty Island.

One legend stands out from all the others. Dating back to the Civil War, it is Poverty Island's most popular sunken treasure tale. *The Beacher* newspaper reported that in 1865, a secret shipment of $4.5 million in gold from France's Emperor Napoleon Bonaparte III was traveling through the Great Lakes and onward down the Mississippi River to help fund Confederate efforts in the South. As the vessel neared Poverty Island, Canadian pirates attacked the ship, murdered the crew, and burned the vessel. Some people believe Union forces learned of the shipment and attacked the French vessel. As in similar legends, the captain took quick measures to protect the loot, ordering his sailors to chain together the five chests of gold and toss them overboard to recover later. However, there is no official record of the attack or of the recovery of riches by either crew members, Union forces, or Confederate supporters.

In the summer of 1933, the eleven-year-old lightkeeper's son watched from the beach as a group of divers searched for the legendary treasure chests thought to lie below the surface near the isle. According to a 2001 article in *The Beacher*, the multiyear treasure hunt funded by Chicago investors was conducted from the *Captain Lawrence*, a two-masted schooner-yacht built in Green Bay in 1898 and owned by Milwaukee resident Wilfred Behrens, an avid shipwreck hunter. Records reveal the 39-ton ship was 60.8 feet long with a 16-foot beam and had a four-man crew.

In 2007 the *Traverse City Record-Eagle* provided an account of how the lightkeeper's young son watched Behrens' crew raise and lower a rustic diving bell off the vessel's deck and into the lake. One day, the boy observed the men shouting and dancing when the bell was raised and then afterward clinking their beer bottles in ecstatic toasts. Their celebratory behavior led Jessen to believe the divers had found something very valuable. But their good fortune was short-lived. A brutal storm hit that very night, and although the crew escaped with their lives, the *Captain Lawrence* was demolished by Mother Nature's fury and whatever treasure it had on board went down with the ship. Young Jessen never saw the treasure hunters again.

The Beacher reported that the Behrens family history maintains the treasure hunter returned to the dive site several times in later years, but he could not raise the necessary funds for a comprehensive search. He died in 1959 without completing his quest.

Then, in 1969, *Skin Diver* magazine published Jessen's story of the strange celebration onboard the *Captain Lawrence,* stirring new interest in Lake Michigan's real-life treasure island. The article attracted a flurry of upwards of two thousand divers to the area, hoping to find and recover the chests of gold, which today would be valued at $500 million or more.

Probably none of the divers have demonstrated more determination than Richard Bennett, a resident of Wauwatosa, Wisconsin, who dedicated three decades to solving the mystery of Poverty Island's lost gold. Bennett's long search for the riches has garnered much national media attention and was the subject of a 1994 episode of NBC's *Unsolved Mysteries,* which unleashed Poverty Island's legend to an entirely new generation of treasure hunters.

Bennett's resolve to recover Poverty Island's gold also brought out his inner inventor, generating even more media recognition. *Popular Mechanics* named his treasure-hunting submarine among the "Top 10 Coolest Backyard Inventions of 2008." A professional diver and retired owner of a scuba training center, Bennett invested $28,000 in the construction of his four-man wet-sub, christened *Jason 300.* According to his website, the fiberglass sub, which he built over a couple summers, is 14 feet long and weighs 525 pounds, is powered by two car batteries, and has headlights that once served

Treasure hunter Richard Bennett tows his homemade sub in preparation for a dive to search for the lost treasure of Poverty Island.

as aircraft landing lights. Using wet suits and diving gear to breathe, the treasure hunter and his crew are able to cover more territory faster using the underwater vessel. To Bennett's disappointment, the sub was not an effective search tool and was subsequently retired.

Despite years of fruitless efforts to locate the gold, Bennett hasn't given up on treasure quests and currently lectures on the subject. He writes on his website, "I have spent thirty-five years or so looking for this treasure. I have also spent thousands of dollars on trips to Door County, Wisconsin. I have frozen my butt off, and have gone without food or water for days while trapped on Poverty Island. I have driven thirty-plus miles from Milwaukee to our entry point in Michigan until I know the tar bumps in the road by heart. To date, I haven't found the key that will open the magic door.

Hidden in a drawer or file cabinet somewhere is a piece of paper with the location of this vast treasure."

One clue—tucked away in an old book, pasted to the back of a painting, or locked in an old safe—could solve the puzzle. However, Steven Libert, a diver and federal government analyst from Virginia, isn't putting his hopes on such a clue miraculously appearing, nor is he waiting for someone to come forth with a new piece of information. Like Bennett, Libert has patiently, steadfastly, and strategically plotted to recover what Lake Michigan has stubbornly held in her cold grip for so long.

A 2001 *Beacher* newspaper article states that Libert located a descendent and legal heir of Behrens, who subsequently sold his rights to the *Captain Lawrence* to Libert's salvage company, Fairport International Exploration. Libert also enlisted Behrens' grandson as a company member.

Libert's mission to discover whether young Jessen's interpretation of the euphoric crew having discovered treasure in 1933 was true prompted him to seek legal ownership of the sunken vessel (and its gold). In the court case of Fairport International Inc. versus the Shipwrecked Vessel *Captain Lawrence* and State of Michigan, documents relate how Libert uncovered debris he believed came from the *Captain Lawrence:* a propeller blade in 1984 and an anchor in 1985. The items sat close to shore off Poverty Island, just forty to sixty feet below the water's surface. Filings in the case further reveal that Wilfred Behrens formally stated on August 16, 1933, that the vessel was bound to Summer Island when a storm blew up, and although the crew survived, the vessel sank near Poverty Island. Three months later, in November 1933, Behrens filed a "Records of Casualties to Vessels" alleging there was no cargo onboard at the time the vessel sank and that the loss totaled $200. Because the Michigan court believed technology existed during Behrens' lifetime to recover the ship, it ruled Behrens had abandoned the ship, thus, the vessel and its contents belonged to the state under the terms of the Abandoned Shipwreck Act of 1987. The Act was designed to preserve submerged cultural resources ranging from schooners and steamships to modern steel vessels, abandoned docks, and prehistoric Native American villages.

Libert's case made its way to the United States Supreme Court, which in 1999 ruled that the lower courts had applied incorrect standards in determining abandonment, but the Grand Rapids District Court refused to rehear the case. Nevertheless, Libert's treasure-hunting saga continued. *The Beacher* reports the diver saying that he and his diving companions found a chest the size of a breadbox on the *Captain Lawrence* deck in July 2000. "It was close enough to touch. And these other guys were shouting at me through our intercom. We had an underwater argument going some 85 feet down."

Libert insisted on settling ownership legally. In 2001, his attempt went before the 6th US Circuit Court of Appeals in Cincinnati, Ohio, which sided with Michigan, closing the case for good—but not Libert's thirst for mythical treasure. In fact, it only provided practice for a greater legal battle involving the State of Michigan and the Republic of France.

In 2004, *Cyber Diver News Network* recounted Libert's possible, if accidental, discovery of one of the Great Lakes' most elusive shipwrecks. It was the underwater explorer's last dive of the 2001 season. He was diving in murky waters at an undisclosed site just west of Poverty Island at a depth of about one hundred feet, where visibility was a mere three inches. While swimming near the bottom, he collided with a long object protruding from the lake bed. Libert claims he didn't know at the time what he had encountered, but he sent up a marker for the crew to note the position using a global positioning device. As so often happens on the Great Lakes, a storm quickly moved in, forcing Libert to wait until the next season to explore his curious find. Thanks to the accurate notation of the location, however, he was not worried about relocating the artifact the next season. Then he would answer the question as to whether the object was from a wrecked vessel of consequence.

It is estimated that more than five thousand ships have found their final resting place in the Great Lakes. The inland seas' sudden storms, gale-force winds, fog, and heavy maritime traffic were a threat to even the largest ships. Once downed, the cold fresh water of the Great Lakes creates the world's best preserved shipwrecks, offering astounding detail and an intimate look into yesterday's maritime culture.

When Libert returned to the marked dive site, he used infrared video to document the discovery, believing he had found the bowsprit of *Le Griffon*—the "Holy Grail of the Great Lakes." Libert's hunch gained credence in 2006, when carbon dating suggested the artifact dated to the same general time period as the *Griffon*.

The *Griffon*, a true archeological and historic treasure, was built more than three hundred years ago for the French explorer Rene-Robert Cavelier, Sieur de La Salle's expedition to find the passage to the Far East and to trade furs. It was the first European vessel to sail the Upper Great Lakes. As a quote from Libert on the La Salle-Griffon Project website says, "The ship is a time capsule that will fill in the missing gaps of La Salle's early exploration of North America."

According to the website, the vessel was built about three miles above the Niagara River with timber cut on site, although speculation remains as to whether construction took place on the American or Canadian side of the falls. The ship featured three masts, a foremast, main and mizzen, and several sails. Armed with two cannons and three rail guns, the ship was designed both to transport soldiers and to supply La Salle's mission from Niagara to Illinois.

The *Griffon*'s maiden voyage took place August 7, 1679, with sixteen men. The website describes the ship's travels, stating it sailed across Lake Erie to its first destination, Detroit, where five more men boarded for the journey to St. Ignace, located near Mackinac Straits. The next stop was Green Bay, Wisconsin. There, La Salle enlisted a six-man crew to return *Le Griffon* to Niagara, where they would gather more men and supplies to construct a fort and an additional ship. Winds were light and conditions favorable on September 18, 1679, as the ship set sail from Washington Island with a cargo of furs to accomplish its new mission. Then, the *Griffon* seemingly vanished from the face of the planet. Some speculate it met its demise in a sudden storm; others speculate it went down in an attack by unfriendly natives or by mutiny. Libert's previous years of research led him to theorize the ship had sunk intact in the northern waters, at the hands of either a violent conflict or a fierce storm. If the wreck is identified as La Salle's *Griffon,* Libert likely will have been the first man to set eyes on the historic vessel in 331 years.

Energized by the possibilities, the modern explorer founded and became president of a new organization, the Great Lakes Exploration Group (GLEG). The group was established to identify, salvage, and preserve the priceless historical artifact. The first hurdle for GLEG was to gain legal authority for its mission. Once again, Libert was up against the Abandoned Shipwreck Act of 1987, which gives the State of Michigan claim over all abandoned shipwrecks in its waters. This time, international maritime law also came into play under the rule that a vessel owned by a government is not abandoned unless that government declares it as such. France, in this instance, was unwilling to relinquish interest in the *Griffon*.

Six years of litigation took place between the diving group and the state. In 2009, France entered the case, claiming ownership, adding to the complexity of issues. It wasn't until the summer of 2010 that the three sides reached agreement. The hard-won agreement allowed Libert's private diving group to proceed with a site assessment, while the US District Court for the Western District of Michigan continues to protect the heritage site.

Meanwhile, the *Canadian Press* reported that Michigan "won't stand in the way of France taking ownership of it if it is the *Griffon*." The article goes on to state that should the wreck be confirmed as La Salle's ship, France desires the ship to be recovered, studied, and displayed in the United States.

Under the official court agreement, GLEG had exclusive, five-year rights to use project data for commercial purposes, including books, videos, films, and audio recordings. Once the agreement was secured, Libert and his partners wasted no time in moving forward, and phase two of the archaeological investigation was soon launched.

The Center for Maritime and Underwater Resource Management (CMURM), based in Laingsburg, Michigan, was a partner in the endeavor to identify Libert's find. A nonprofit scientific and educational organization, CMURM's impressive client list includes the National Park Service and the National Trust for Historic Preservation. CMURM's role in the investigation was to determine the nature of the recovered artifacts, including time period, type of vessel, national affiliation, and other identifying details.

This detective work is a far cry from the rustic diving bell Jessen watched the *Captain Lawrence* crew use in 1933 in their attempts to recover Poverty Island's sunken gold. The two-year *Griffon* study deployed sophisticated high-resolution acoustic imaging tools to determine what might be buried beneath lake sediment. Some of the same tools employed in the Lake Michigan operation were used to discover the iconic *Titanic* at the Atlantic Ocean bottom. CMURM also used an autonomous underwater vehicle with digital cameras to produce images of the site. Scientific divers had the capacity to document details of the submerged ship with high-resolution acoustic imaging tools. Based on those findings, a site analysis was completed in 2011. The final phase of this quest for La Salle's *Griffon* included a test excavation.

The host port for the expedition and investigation is the city of Charlevoix, where Libert owns a home. This popular Lake Michigan harbor town in northwest Michigan, from which his quest for the historic ship continues, is eighty miles from where the *Griffon* last set sail.

According to the *Door County Pulse*, Libert's team planned to restart the search in 2018.

Scientists from some of the world's most prestigious institutions are watching and participating in the mission to validate and excavate *Le Griffon*. If Libert and his associates successfully solve the disappearance of La Salle's famed ship, Michigan is destined to become the site of the country's most important maritime archaeological find. And Poverty Island may have a chance to change its name to something more befitting an isle harboring such a valuable cultural treasure.

CHAPTER 2

The Mysterious Disappearance of Jimmy Hoffa

Anxious and frustrated, Jimmy dropped a coin into a pay-phone to dial his wife at their Lake Orion home north of Detroit. It was mid-afternoon, July 30, 1975. Cars rushed along Telegraph Road, intensifying the summer heat as Jimmy placed the call from near the Machus Red Fox restaurant in Bloomfield Township. Dressed in a golf shirt and loafers, few people would have recognized the man standing at the payphone as one of America's most powerful figures.

Jimmy had walked to the public phone from the restaurant parking lot, where he was to meet reputed mobsters Anthony Provenzano (Tony Pro) of New Jersey and Anthony Giacalone (Tony Jack) of Detroit. Anyone who had dealings with the labor leader knew Jimmy demanded punctuality. When the Tonys didn't show, he called home to ask his wife, Josephine, whether there were any messages left for him. Did he have the meeting time wrong? The brief conversation was the couple's last.

At 3:30 p.m., Jimmy phoned a family friend and related that he had been stood up by the men. That was the last time anyone heard from Jimmy Hoffa, a man whose entire life seemed characterized by paradox.

More than four decades have passed since Jimmy Hoffa's mysterious disappearance. While the one-time president of the International Brotherhood of Teamsters was presumed dead, his body has never been found and no one was has ever been charged with a crime in relation to his disappearance.

The search for the missing Hoffa was one of the most extensive ever conducted. Only hours after Jimmy's disappearance, the Detroit FBI Bureau had 225 agents searching for the labor leader. Millions of dollars were spent on the investigation, which eventually resulted in 16,000 pages of FBI documents, but there were no clear answers or arrests.

Why were so many resources invested in the attempt to solve Hoffa's disappearance? In his book *Digging for the Truth: The Final Resting Place of Jimmy Hoffa,* Jeffrey Scott Hansen writes, "He was so powerful that with a single phone call he could shut down just about every trucking company, warehouse, and shipyard operating in the United States."

At the union's peak of power, almost two million workers joined forces as Teamsters, thanks in large part to Jimmy Hoffa's leadership. Speculation of his ties to organized crime and government authorities added to both his mystique and the extraordinary influence he thrived upon. Whether Jimmy Hoffa was a hero of the American worker or a brutal labor boss depends on one's point of view.

According to a *Time* magazine report, Hoffa, sixty-two at the time of his disappearance, left Lake Orion at about 1:00 p.m. and drove alone to the upscale restaurant he often frequented and where he expected to meet the Tonys to resolve escalating differences. Witnesses in the Red Fox parking lot reported that Jimmy got into a car, seemingly voluntarily, and drove away with Charles (Chuckie) O'Brien and two alleged mobsters for what was likely his last ride.

Known for his short temper and tough manner, James Riddle Hoffa—even his middle name forewarns of intrigue—was born in Indiana on a day of love, Valentine's Day, 1913. After his father's death when Jimmy was twelve, his mother moved the family to a working class neighborhood in west Detroit. Like many youth of the era, Jimmy dropped out of school by the ninth grade and took a job to help support the family. When the Great Depression hit, hard times grew harder. The teen worked several jobs during this period, but it was his stint as a dock worker for the Kroger Food Company that sealed his destiny. There, workers were forced to wait without pay for deliveries or lose their jobs.

"One of Hoffa's foremen was a tyrant who browbeat the workers for no reason and fired them just because he could," Hansen writes. "Men like this were commonplace. They enjoyed playing God to those who could not fight back and epitomized the term bully."

Hansen further documents how one day an outraged Jimmy led the dock workers in refusing to load crates of strawberries unless management heard workers' grievances. The *Detroit News* reported that after several days of negotiating with Kroger management,

Hoffa and his supporters scored a victory that increased the workers' hourly wage from thirty-two cents to forty-five cents, a guarantee of at least a half day's wage per day, insurance, and recognition of their union.

Hoffa's lifelong mission soon became defined as a fight to win a living wage, adequate working conditions, and a decent pension for American workers. The means to that end came on Hoffa's terms, as he feared no one—not the mob, big business, or government officials, all of which at times wanted to see Jimmy erased from the picture.

Between 1937 and 1957, Jimmy's power within the labor union grew. With police on their side, companies would often use muscle to crush worker discontent. Jimmy fought back by developing associations with some unseemly characters.

The *Detroit News* quoted Hoffa's account of the period, "The police were no help. They would beat your brains in for even talking union. The cops harassed us every day. If you went on strike, you got your head broken."

The newspaper further reported that Jimmy was beaten by police or strikebreakers twenty-four times in his first year as business agent for Teamsters Local 299 and thrown in jail countless times.

In 1952, Jimmy's star rose when he was elected the union's international vice president. Only one year later, he became president of the Central Conference, negotiating for twenty Midwestern and Southern states.

As time passed, violence escalated among rival unions and the heat from the government accelerated, namely in the form of

Robert Kennedy, chief counsel for the famous McClellan Hearings. The crackdown on labor racketeering and government pressure led to Teamsters' President Dave Beck's prosecution on embezzlement and labor racketeering and conviction for income tax evasion. Now, the door was open for Jimmy to become the international president. It was 1957.

Although Jimmy escaped conviction during those years, he, too, was in deep—"involving everything from pension fund skimming, to extortion and murder," as Hansen noted. Federal investigations haunted Jimmy throughout the 1950s and 1960s. New battle lines were drawn when Robert Kennedy was named US Attorney General by his brother President John F. Kennedy.

The battle broke out in 1962, after a jailed Teamster made a deal with prosecutors that led to Hoffa being charged with accepting an illegal payment from an employer. Hoffa was acquitted only to be convicted two years later of jury tampering and sentenced to eight years in prison. He was sentenced to an additional five years when Chicago authorities convicted him of fraud and conspiracy related to the handling of the union benefits fund.

Many believed Hoffa was railroaded. The *Detroit News* reported Supreme Court Justice Earl Warren calling the jury-tampering conviction "an affront to the quality and fairness of federal law enforcement."

In 2009, forty-five years after Hoffa's conviction, Cleveland State University retired law professor William Tabac sought to determine whether the Justice Department led by Robert Kennedy illegally gathered evidence against Hoffa in the jury-tampering case. The files were unsealed by US District Judge Todd

J. Campbell in Nashville, Tennessee. What they revealed surprised even Tabac.

CBS News reported the files show the Grand Jury testimony of Justice Department Official Walter J. Sheridan indicated, "Associates of the late Teamsters' boss Jimmy Hoffa plotted to ambush a group of FBI agents during his 1962 trial in Nashville." The plan was not carried out, and the testimony did not indicate whether Hoffa knew of the scheme, although it served to further Hoffa's prosecution in the 1964 jury-tampering case.

The reopened files were redacted, incomplete, and inconclusive, and although they shed more light on the face-off between the Attorney General and Hoffa, the files failed to prove Kennedy's guilt or to disprove Hoffa's.

Jimmy's bitter relationship with the Kennedys ran deep. Some suggest Hoffa is linked, along with the mob, to the Kennedy assassinations as well as to the 1961 mob/CIA Bay of Pigs invasion, an assassination attempt on Fidel Castro and the planned overthrow of the Cuban government.

In March 1967, Jimmy began serving his thirteen-year sentence at Pennsylvania's Lewisburg Federal Prison. Teamsters' Vice President Frank Fitzsimmons was left in charge of union business. This shift in leadership drove a complex chain of events that eventually led to Jimmy's dramatic end. Tony Pro, later a key suspect in Hoffa's disappearance, served time at Lewisburg alongside Jimmy and was vice president for Teamsters Local 560 in Union City, New Jersey. Hansen's book recounts the bitter dispute that arose between the two union leaders during their prison term. According to Hansen, Tony Pro wanted Hoffa's

Jimmy Hoffa orders wildcat strikers back to work at a 1966 gathering at Cobo Hall in Detroit.

help in securing a hefty Teamster pension upon his release. Hoffa refused.

In his book, *I Heard You Paint Houses,* author Charles Brandt quotes mob hit man Frank "The Irishman" Sheeran retelling a prison incident from the period: "Pro said something about ripping Jimmy's guts out. I heard the guards had to break it up. From that day to the day they both died, Jimmy hated Pro and Pro hated Jimmy more."

On December 23, 1971, after President Richard Nixon received $500,000 (technically for his reelection fund), the president commuted Jimmy's sentence. Jimmy walked out of Lewisburg the same day. Once free, Jimmy channeled his energy toward rebuilding his union flanks. Earlier in 1971, he had relinquished his position as union president, allowing for the election of Fitzsimmons to the office. Jimmy was determined to regain the union presidency. If reports are accurate, Nixon's coffers grew considerably as a result of the Hoffa incarceration. Hansen writes, "He had appointed Frank Fitzsimmons, who he thought was his loyal lackey, to be his successor until he was able to get out of prison. What Hoffa did not count on was Fitzsimmons' involvement with Tony Provenzano to pay a large sum of money to President Nixon to place in the pardon that Hoffa 'does not engage in direct or indirect management of any labor organization until March of 1980.'"

Jimmy claimed he had no knowledge of the prohibitive clause when he signed the pardon and that it was later added illegally. He launched a court battle to have the stipulation dropped and was confident he would prevail in the case. Brandt's book reveals Sheeran's claim that although Sheeran did not know the source, he delivered $270,000 in a clandestine drop to then Attorney General John Mitchell in exchange for an affidavit refuting legality of restrictions on Jimmy's labor activities.

Meanwhile, certain organized crime members who were unhappy with Jimmy's vow to clean up the union built their own campaign against him. In the book *The Strange Disappearance of Jimmy Hoffa,* authors Charles Ashman and Rebecca Sobel state that organized crime viewed the Teamster Pension Fund as a bank where they could easily borrow clean money to set up legitimate businesses. In the mid-1970s, their private golden goose is believed to have held $1.5 billion in total assets and real estate loans amounting to about $800 million. Certain mob factions found Fitzsimmons more accommodating than Jimmy, despite Jimmy's cooperation during previous years. Sheeran told Brandt that Jimmy grew reckless with public statements regarding his intention to free the union from mob influence.

Sheeran, a trusted Hoffa associate, claimed he warned the labor leader of the mob's increasing hostility toward Jimmy's clean campaign, specifically Russell Bufalino, one of history's most powerful Mafia leaders and onetime Hoffa ally. Sheeran said that months before Jimmy's disappearance, Jimmy was told he would be hit if he didn't back down from his pursuit to regain union presidency. Jimmy never backed down from a fight and wasn't about to begin then.

And so the mystery of July 30, 1975, quietly unfolded. In a deathbed confession, Sheeran admitted to Brandt that Bufalino had sent him to Detroit, where a car was waiting for him. He said he was instructed to drive to a modest house at 17841 Beaverland Street, located in an unassuming neighborhood near the Red Fox restaurant, where Sheeran said he met two men he identified as gangsters. According to the self-proclaimed hit man, Tony Pro and

Tony Jack, who Jimmy was to meet, had established airtight alibis for a devious death plan that was detailed down to the minute. Brandt quoted Sheeran saying, "Everything was going to be very close to everything else, all of it a straight shoot. You most definitely couldn't go driving around any distance and making lots of turns with Jimmy's body in the car."

The account in Brandt's book states Teamster Charles "Chuckie" O'Brien was at the wheel of the car that pulled into the Red Fox parking lot. O'Brien was raised by Hoffa and his wife after his mother's death. Sheeran and an associate of Tony Pro were also in the car with Chuckie. Jimmy walked up to the car, angry for being made to wait. Chuckie and Sheeran, two people Jimmy trusted, convinced him to get in the car, according to Sheeran's confession. They all arrived back at the Beaverland Street house within minutes, and Jimmy entered the front door with his longtime associate, Sheeran. Jimmy quickly recognized the situation was a set up, and while he rushed to escape through the front door, Sheeran shot the labor leader twice in the back of the head.

Sheeran's story, which he had relayed to Brandt over several years, described how Jimmy was placed in a body bag, taken out the back door, and transported by car for immediate cremation at a facility with mob connections. Ashman and Sobel lay out the initial investigation timeline in their book. They report that at 7:20 the morning following Jimmy's scheduled meeting, family friends went to the Red Fox, where they found his abandoned car. By 8:15 a.m., local police were at the scene. At 2:00 p.m., state police were brought in and the FBI was alerted. At suppertime, Jimmy's son, James P. Hoffa, filed a missing persons report, and by the evening of July 31, the entire world knew Jimmy Hoffa was missing.

A full-scale nationwide search for Jimmy was soon underway, and $300,000 in reward money was put up by the family, friends, and the union. Hundreds of tips came in to law enforcement, and hundreds of individuals were interviewed by authorities. But investigations failed to offer any hope of an arrest.

The Ashman and Sobel book states: "Two weeks had passed since the Hoffa disappearance and law enforcement agencies were issuing gloomy reports. The FBI, although they still had more than a hundred agents checking around the country, also admitted they could come up with nothing new."

Ashman and Sobel report that, in September 1971, authorities jumped on what they thought was finally a solid lead and organized a massive weeklong dig on a swampy plot of land in Waterford Township, located minutes from the Red Fox. The dig drew a crowd of spectators but nothing to solve the mystery. No official reports surfaced as a result of the investigation.

On September 3, 2002, seventeen years after Jimmy's disappearance, the State of Michigan closed the Hoffa file. But the case refused to die. In 2004, authorities searched the Beaverland Street home Sheeran had implicated as the site of the crime. Although homicide investigators found traces of blood, the DNA did not match Jimmy's and the search failed to provide viable clues.

In 2006, *USA Today* reported another major FBI search, this time involving archaeologists and anthropologists at Hidden Dreams Farm in Milford Township. Located less than an hour's drive northwest of Detroit, the farm was known as a former mob meeting place and was previously owned by a Teamster. It was originally searched in the 1970s, but this time heavy equipment and cadaver dogs were brought in, yet it failed to turn up a body or further clues.

In 2009, *ABC News* reported on a search believed to be yet another for the missing Hoffa, this one at a Detroit lumberyard. FBI agents fenced off the site and hung tarp to prevent public viewing of the operation. No reports surfaced as a result of this investigation.

Everyone had a theory as to what happened to Jimmy. On a website dedicated to Mafia stories, Thom L. Jones listed several of the more popular conjectures on the union leader's disappearance:

- Dumped into the AuSable River in thirty feet of water between two dams
- Put through a mob-operated fat-rendering plant that was burned down
- Buried under the helicopter pad at the Sheraton Savannah Resort Hotel
- Crushed in a steel compactor for junk cars at Central Sanitation Services, a company in Hamtramck owned by Raffaele Quasarano and destroyed by fire in 1978 (part of the site was later occupied by the Wayne County Jail)
- Stuffed into a fifty-gallon oil drum and taken on a Gateway Transportation truck to the Gulf of Mexico
- Ground up in little pieces and dumped into a Florida swamp
- Buried in a field in Waterford Township

- Disposed of in the Central Waste Management trash incinerator at Hamtramck, owned by Peter Vitale and Raffaele Quasarano
- Buried at the bottom of a swimming pool behind a mansion in Bloomfield Hills
- Buried under a public works garage in Cadillac, Michigan
- Dumped into a one-hundred-acre gravel pit near Highland owned by his brother

One of the more colorful theories regarding Jimmy's final resting place is the claim that he was buried beneath the Giants Stadium in East Rutherford, New Jersey. In 2010, when the stadium was slated for demolition, the Associated Press reported that the legend was resurrected. The article states, "The west end zone became the Jimmy Hoffa Memorial End Zone. Teams didn't just beat the Giants or Jets, they Jimmy Hoffa-ed them." The article also quotes retired FBI agent Jim Kossler recalling how contractors unearthed several corpses during the stadium's construction, but none were Jimmy's. Stadium demolition was completed as scheduled and without a Hoffa search.

Is that the end of the story? Maybe not. New cadaver sensing technology developed by the National Institute of Standards and Technology could detect Jimmy's body, even beneath the concrete parking lot now located at the former Giants stadium site, according to a Discovery Channel News report.

Despite the millions of dollars and thousands of man hours spent investigating Jimmy Hoffa's disappearance over the years, it remains one of America's most intriguing cases. Today, most of the principal players in the drama of Jimmy's life are themselves long buried, taking with them the truth of his final hours. Whether the mystery surrounding his disappearance is ever uncovered and regardless of how one views Hoffa's tactics, few would dispute that James Riddle Hoffa helped to improve the quality of life for millions of American workers and their families through his work to establish a fair wage and humane working conditions for workers.

CHAPTER 3

Michigan's Mini Stonehenge

When Terri Bussey stepped onto Beaver Island at Saint James Harbor in the summer of 1985, she had no inkling her visit would launch a decades-long controversy.

Beaver Island is the largest island on Lake Michigan and the largest of the seven-island Beaver archipelago, and the only isle in the chain with commerce. Situated thirty-two miles off the shores of the city of Charlevoix in the northwest corner of the Lower Peninsula, the isle is just twelve miles long and six miles wide and home to only six hundred residents.

Bussey, who is part Chippewa and served as director of the Grand Rapids Inter-Tribal Council's Michigan Indian Press, had come to the island to hunt for Native American artifacts, hoping to learn more about the roots of her people. What Bussey discovered on her fateful summer trip to the isle eventually led some experts to conclude that human habitation of Beaver Island predated Columbus and may go back as far as six thousand years. Others continue to dispute her discovery as a random act of nature.

Native Americans are documented to have set foot on the isle 2,200 years ago. However, local Ottawa oral history accounts for a tribal presence on the island dating back only three hundred years, sometime in the mid-1700s. The Ottawa are believed to have settled the isle to escape the encroachment of white settlers on Michigan's mainland. Beaver Island would have been a friendly place for the tribe. Its woodlands, wildlife, and rich fishery likely provided a bountiful sustenance. Like their ancient predecessors, who may have been wiped out by pestilence or simply decided not to linger on the secluded island, the more modern tribe would have enjoyed an abundance of deer, nuts, and berries.

Beaver Island's history took a strange twist in 1848, when Mormon James Strang settled a colony on the isle. Strang, a rival of Brigham Young who was competing for control of the religious sect, crowned himself king of Beaver Island. The move established the island as the only monarchy to ever exist in America. But Strang's reign was short-lived. In 1856, he was assassinated by disgruntled followers only a few feet from the Mormon Print Shop where his religious tracts were printed. At the time of his murder, a US Navy ship, the USS *Michigan,* was docked nearby in Saint James Harbor. Following the crime, its captain took custody of the assassins and transported them to Mackinac Island, where they were celebrated as heroes and set free.

The Mormons were run off Beaver Island during the 1850s and replaced by Irish settlers who dubbed the spot "America's Emerald Isle." Island legend maintains the Irish took advantage of the Mormons' sudden departure, using furniture, tools, and other objects they left behind.

During the latter part of the century, Beaver Island's economy prospered. It was the nation's largest supplier of freshwater fish until 1893, when overfishing brought the industry to a halt. By the early 1900s, though, island commerce had rebounded by capitalizing on logging and tourism.

Tourism on the peaceful Lake Michigan haven thrived and now represents the cornerstone of the island's economy. With its long stretches of golden sand beaches, lush hardwood and pine forests, and quaint village, the remote island looks much the same as it did the day Bussey stepped foot there to hunt for artifacts.

Bussey combed for pieces of pottery and arrowheads at the island's west side, off Mrs. Reddings Road (named for the woman who had once lived at the road's end) and below Angeline's Bluff (named after Angeline Wabaninkee). Even today, island maps refer to the road and bluff by these names. It was near this area that Indian artifacts dating back 500 to 1,200 years have been found. Later, a group of ancestors of the Grand Traverse Band of Ottawa and Chippewa Indians of Peshawbestown in Leelanau County established a camp in the area. The inland site sits adjacent to Reddings Road and features dry, sandy soil covered with underbrush and a profusion of ferns. Forest surrounds the wide clearing, offering a sense of seclusion. Silence blankets the site. The only sound heard is the whisper of wind rushing through the woods.

While forging through underbrush a few feet from the gravel road, Bussey came upon a unique boulder measuring about four feet high by five feet across featuring a hole the size of a basketball in the center of the top surface. Soon after the discovery, the *Detroit News* reported that Bussey believed early occupants of the island had used a stone tool to chisel the hole into the rock and to etch into it "what appeared to be a man-made grid." Another stone is said to have the image of a sheaf of feathers carved into it.

Her curiosity awakened, Bussey investigated further. She paced off from the rock to compass points, and what she learned astonished her. Using the compass, she located several more boulders and rocks rising from the earth; smaller ones sat partially buried and hidden in underbrush or moss. Irregular in shape and color, they ranged from two to ten feet in diameter. Bussey's rocks, thirty-nine in all, formed a circle 397 feet in diameter.

Bussey sensed she had stumbled onto something significant, but she didn't know exactly what. For two nights she camped at the site. Under the night sky, she found an unmistakable connection between the boulder placements and star positions, convincing her the site contained secrets of the past.

Until 1985, the primary evidence suggesting ancient inhabitation of Beaver Island had been the discovery of three pre-Columbian mounds investigated by Henry Gillman in 1871. His excavation had uncovered stone awls, axes, hoes, and other tools. Gillman reported that these implements were skillfully constructed. However, academics disputed the possibility of ancient island settlers and old world immigrants in Michigan prior to Columbus.

Was Bussey's intriguing stone circle built by her Native American ancestors in centuries past or by ancient citizens thousands of years earlier? Substantial evidence suggests the latter. The Eastern Woodland Indians were not known for building stone monuments. The rocks used to construct Beaver Island's stone circle also would have had to have been moved to the site and positioned, a difficult task considering the size of the larger ring boulders. Certain tribal members claim the organic matter beneath some of the stones indicates the land was burned for clearing before the stones were set, furthering the theory that the circle is more than an accident of nature.

In her book *Michigan Prehistory Mysteries,* Betty Sodders refers to a stone hammer on display at the Beaver Island History Museum. She notes that it is similar to ones thought to be used by copper miners four thousand years ago on the Upper Peninsula's Keweenaw Peninsula. Sodders writes, "Professionally, there has been speculation over the years that Beaver Island was a way-station for those enigmatic ancient people that carried out the copper trade."

The island historical museum also displays a stone ax similar to objects found in Ireland, suggesting a Celtic tie, according to Sodders. Beaver Island's stone circle is often called a mini Stonehenge, referring to the prehistoric monument in England that scientists believe was constructed about 2500 to 2200 BC. In his book *Mystic Michigan: Part Three,* Mark Jagar notes that some geologists attest to the theory of a super continent and that before the continents split, Michigan was located at the continent's north central position at about the same latitude as the iconic Stonehenge. He also points out that Bible scholars date the Great Flood to about 2000 BC, suggesting Beaver Island's stone circle was created by a civilization succumbing to doom in the catastrophic flood event.

Sodders discloses that some archaeologists attribute stone rings found across the United States to people of the Mississippian culture called the mound builders. Their civilization encompassed an area from Lake Superior to the Gulf of Mexico and from the Mississippi River to the Carolinas. Historians separate the civilization into periods: Emergent Mississipian, AD 800–1000; Early Woodland, AD 950–1050; Middle Woodland, AD 1050–1300; and the Late Woodland period, AD 1350–1581. The mound builders are believed to have migrated to Michigan during the middle phase, about AD 1200.

Excited about her discovery, Bussey shared her find with archaeologists and members of the nearby Grand Traverse Band of Ottawa and Chippewa Indians. To her dismay, archaeologists dismissed her mini Stonehenge as glacial debris left by geological changes. It wasn't until some time later, when she captured the interest of Dr. Donald Heldman, the director of archaeology for Mackinac Island Park Commission who was working at Fort Michilimackinac in Mackinaw City, that the stone circle received serious study. Heldman was the first expert to confirm that the stone configuration had been constructed by humans, according to Sodders.

News of Michigan's Stonehenge spread. In 1988, University of Wisconsin professor Dr. James Scherz visited the site. Scherz, an expert in pre-Columbian history of Wisconsin and Michigan copper culture, documented the configuration as a possible calendar. A note accompanying his calculations reads: "The orientation is a mirror image of what we see, as if the stars of the crystal sphere surrounding the earth were viewed from afar."

Ancients who devised stone circles used them to chart the course of a twelve-month period. The sun moves across the horizon; a short distance is measured each day. On the autumn equinox

(September 21) and the spring equinox (March 21), the sun rises due east and sets due west, reversing the process every half year on the solstice (December and June 21). An object on the ground aligned with another object creates shadows that function as a guide to the seasons, providing an effective solar calendar.

Scherz notes on his sketched diagram of the stone circle: "The possible calendar function here, as at many other sites in northern regions, focuses on the fall cross quarter day in late October (our Halloween) and terminates in late November, as if people who once used this site left by that time. Further south, the focus is on the winter solstice."

In 2005, a colleague of Scherz, Archie Eschborn, author of two books on an underwater prehistoric site in Wisconsin, made an expedition to Beaver Island's stone circle to see what connection it might have to the Wisconsin Rock Lake site across Lake Michigan. Eschborn reported in an article appearing in *Astrea Magazine* that Native American elders considered the island's stone circle a sacred spot placed by the "Ancient Ones," but that no living Native American knew why.

Some speculate the large hole carved in the center rock was devised to hold a pole for celestial readings, according to Eschborn's magazine article. Eschborn disagreed, believing it was too shallow to hold a pole of any substantial size. He concluded the hand-hewn hole was an offertory bowl because of its resemblance to other monolithic boulders in which offertory bowls are carved.

What Eschborn found on close examination of the center boulder (as reported in Sodder's book) surprised even those familiar with the site. On a rainy day punctuated by powerful bolts of lightning and rumbles of thunder, Eschborn was accompanied to the stone circle by island historian Bill Cashman. While Eschborn pondered the purpose of the carved bowl and studied the lines etched across the center boulder's surface, he noticed what was unmistakably a relief map of Michigan's Lower Peninsula, something every schoolchild in the state would also recognize. After all, Michiganders at even young ages learn to map the "Mitten State" on the palm of their hands. The boulder's remarkable relief map includes Lake Superior, Lake Michigan, and Lake Huron, as well as land masses of Canada, Minnesota, Wisconsin, and Michigan's Lower and Upper Peninsulas. The map also includes a depiction of the Mississippi River as it would have appeared several millennia ago, according to Eschborn's report. As the researcher stood in awe of the stone map, rain filled the recesses surrounding the mitten, emphasizing the lakes, making the carving even more remarkable.

Eschborn's party proceeded to hunt for a boulder featuring an inscription of "bird wings," as both Heldman and Scherz had documented earlier. The inscription possibly holds a vital link validating the stone circle's original purpose as a map for ancient travelers. The storm cut short the site visit before Eschborn was able to locate the significant markings.

Others also sought to locate these markings. "We were told by Native Americans that ancient 'Thunderbird Lines' intersected at this old ceremonial site," wrote Zecharia Sitchin and Frank Joseph in an article appearing in the book, *Ancient America: Lost History and Legends, Unearthed and Explored.* "They recount how one such line went to the ancient mines on Isle Royal, and another to Rock Lake, Wisconsin." A tribal elder revealed to the researchers that rock structures hidden from view beneath the surface of Rock Lake are associated with rock structures in Madison, Wisconsin, as well as on Beaver Island. "He described the network of rock structures as long-range 'grid lines' set up by wise men in prehistoric times. According to legend, other ancient lines arranged by the Ancients are marked by two giant perched stones near Madison, Chamberlain Rock, and Spirit Rock."

The article notes that north-south alignment would have been visible about two miles apart and can be traced to other sites in Wisconsin and Michigan. This led the writers to conclude: "If this is not all coincidence, it would seem that ancient wise men did indeed create a giant grid system marked by rock structures between prominent recognizable land forms to aid long distance travelers."

Once Bussey uncovered the island's stone circle, the Grand Traverse Band of Ottawa and Chippewa Indians took action to save it from commercial development, protect it from vandalism, and preserve it as a ceremonial site. Islanders cooperated with the effort, keeping Beaver Island's mysterious secret from leaking to the wider public or commercializing on the find. Ironically, the center stone could not be saved from a run-in with a snowplow, according to island historians. Located only a few feet off Reddings Road, the center stone, blanketed by a snowfall, was struck one day by a snowplow driver unaware of the monument. The boulder may have withstood thousands of years of harsh northern Michigan winters and blazing summer suns, but not modern man. The blow from the truck split the round boulder down the middle into two parts. Luckily, its bowl and carved Michigan map

An image carved into the mini Stonehenge's center boulder features an identifiable map of Michigan and the Great Lakes.

remained intact to allow scientists the opportunity to continue to unravel its mystery.

Despite the center stone's split, tribal members continue to make the two-hour ferry journey to the island from the mainland to hold ceremonies at the stone circle. Fire pits show evidence of their recent presence, while the bowls of the center stone and the largest boulder positioned in accordance to the equinoxes hold offerings, as they perhaps did many, many moons ago.

The number of mysterious discoveries by scientists on Beaver Island continues to grow. Findings now include the Angeline Bluff stone circle, seven medicine wheels, several petroglyphs, and ancient raised garden beds. As recently as 2009, a new petroglyph was found on the isle. Area tribal elders told archaeologists that etchings on the stone circle's center boulder led them to discover the medicine wheels but would not offer further explanation. The island's ancient garden beds, additional evidence of an early culture presence on the isle, were reported by W. B. Hinsdale, according to Sodders. Her book reports that the early Michigan garden beds were "symmetrical, low, earth ridges laid out with precision and showed much artistic conception." A century ago, Beaver Island's ancient garden beds were found overgrown with two-hundred-year-old trees, definitive proof of historic, if not prehistoric, origins.

In 2007, a possible link to the ancient Beaver Island riddle emerged in quite an unlikely place. Underwater archaeologists were hired to explore the floor of Grand Traverse Bay, a popular Lake Michigan bay at Traverse City, about fifty miles south of Charlevoix, the launch point for travelers to Beaver Island. According to a *Traverse City-Record Eagle* report, during the survey Dr. Mark Holley, a scientist for the Grand Traverse Bay Underwater Preserve Council, and his team of students found sections of a Civil War–era pier, a shipwreck, and to the divers' astonishment, possible evidence of prehistoric residents.

Holley earned his PhD in underwater archaeology at Scotland's University of Edinburgh, where he was involved in field surveys of prehistoric underwater artificial islet sites located off Scotland's west coast. He later investigated sites in Lake Huron's Thunder Bay and Saginaw Bay and is currently a professor at Northwestern Michigan College in Traverse City.

Holley discovered what he suspected was a stone circle sitting along the sandy floor of the bay at a depth of forty feet. The stones sharply contrasted against the bay's flat bottom, making the formation distinct. Along with the circle of stones ranging in size, divers discovered a granite boulder four feet high by five feet wide with distinct markings Holley believes are a petroglyph. The etchings carved into the boulder's surface provide an image of a mastodon-like figure with a back, hump, head, trunk, tusk, ears, and parts of legs, with a spear in its side. The elephant-like mastodons disappeared from North America ten thousand years ago and are not known to have ranged into northern Michigan.

Are these clues to an ancient people connected to Michigan or to accidents of nature? Holley speculates the stones may have lined the shore six thousand to ten thousand years ago. Others speculate the underwater stone circle was a fishing weir associated with a river long vanished. Many experts are reluctant to acknowledge the find was created by man and are withholding judgment until further proof authenticates the discoveries. Unfortunately, few archaeologists and geologists are also divers, so most are unable to examine the etchings and stone configurations firsthand.

Leaders of the Grand Traverse Band of Ottawa and Chippewa Indians contend that the underwater Stonehenge may have religious significance to the tribe and consider the site sacred. The exact location of the site remains secret out of respect for the tribe and to prevent vandalism while scientists resolve the debate about its origins.

High-tech tools allow site investigations to reveal ever more details about Michigan's stone circles, but decades after Bussey's amazing discovery, there is still no consensus among the scientific community as to the age, purpose, origins, or significance of the curious Beaver Island and Grand Traverse Bay configurations. For now, the Mitten's prehistory remains a cliffhanger waiting for future clues to reveal the plot of the Michigan Stonehenge story.

CHAPTER 4

The Deadly Great Lakes Triangle

M anistique's Thompson Harbor bustled with activity and the scent of pine permeated the air as workers loaded five thousand fresh-cut Christmas trees onto the schooner *Rouse Simmons*. Captain Herman Schuenemann was eager to get the profitable last load of the season to his Chicago customers. Little did he know that the voyage was destined to be his last.

Early November 1912 had brought the most violent storm of the century to the Great Lakes, leaving Christmas tree farms in the Upper Peninsula buried deep in snow. Poor access to the fields created a shortage of the high-demand evergreens. At the same time, Chicagoans at the opposite end of Lake Michigan preparing for festive Victorian era holiday celebrations hoped they would be among the lucky ones to get a tree. Families looked forwarded to coming to the docks to select a tree shipped three hundred miles from Manistique.

On the morning of November 27, the peg-legged, bearded Claud Winters waited along Chicago's Clark Street wharf for his friend and business partner, Herman Schuenemann, to sail the *Rouse Simmons* into the harbor with its green cargo. Claud had men on hand to unload the ship. But Schuenemann, the man known as Captain Santa, his crew of seventeen, and the aging vessel never arrived. In years to come, the "Christmas Tree Ship" gained notoriety as a ghost vessel and a victim of the Great Lakes Triangle.

November is notorious for vicious storms on the Great Lakes. Just days before the *Rouse Simmons* sailed from Manistique, an historically brutal four-day snowstorm had destroyed ten large freighters, taking four hundred sailors to their watery grave. But Captain Schuenemann was a true master of the inland seas. In a previous storm that had damaged or sunk every schooner on Lake Michigan, his was the only one to escape harm. So, the storm brewing on the day of the *Rouse Simmons*'s departure from the Upper Peninsula gave the fearless captain few worries.

Once underway, however, weather conditions deteriorated. By the time the ship passed Sturgeon Bay, Wisconsin, she was flying distress signals. The Lifesaving Service Station sent out a twenty-five-man rescue team into the wild seas to aid her. Despite their best efforts, they were unable to intercept the Christmas Tree Ship, and the ice-covered vessel slipped into a shroud of snow and vanished.

On Christmas Eve, Claud returned to the docks, believing that somehow Captain Santa and the *Rouse Simmons* would appear. He waited in the frigid Chicago night. As dawn broke Christmas morning, police found peg-leg Claud frozen to death—still waiting.

Claud's death didn't end the saga of the Christmas Tree Ship. Five years later, unconfirmed rumors abounded suggesting the Christmas

Tree Ship was still afloat and sailing the lake. In 1918, the SS *Carolina* reported the hulk of a ship drifting in Lake Michigan near Chicago, according to Jay Gourley in his book, *The Great Lakes Triangle*. Some thought it was the *Rouse Simmons* released from Davey Jones' Locker, Gourley wrote. The Coast Guard responded to the report, but a heavy mist thwarted all attempts to find the ghost ship.

The *Rouse Simmons* is one of scores of unexplained wrecks within the region. The *In Search of . . . The Great Lakes Triangle* video series reports that one-third of all unsolved sea and air disasters in America take place within the Great Lakes Triangle. Michigan lies within the heart of this notorious zone. The treacherous Great Lakes Triangle sits between longitudes seventy-six degrees and ninety-two degrees west and forty-one degrees and forty-nine degrees north. Hundreds of baffling events have occurred within these boundaries, even more than within the better known Bermuda Triangle, according to Gourley.

Mysterious disappearances of vessels within the region go far back in history. The region's Native American oral legends tell of a "Great Sturgeon" with the power to create rough seas and monster waves capable of sinking boats. Unexplained disappearances continue today despite the use of sophisticated navigational aids, instrumentation, and warning systems. Time and time again, comprehensive official investigations into the cause of these disappearances and deadly accidents produce no explanation.

The first large ship to sail the Great Lakes, explorer Rene-Robert Cavelier, Sieur de La Salle's *Le Griffon* also became the first ghost ship after it vanished in 1679 without leaving a single clue as to its fate.

The best known ship to disappear within the Great Lakes Triangle in modern times was the SS *Edmund Fitzgerald*. The legendary ore carrier, fondly known as "The Fitz," was the pride of the Great Lakes fleet when it vanished from Lake Superior near Whitefish Point on November 10, 1975. Like the *Griffon,* it was the largest of its kind on the inland seas at the time of its demise. The 729-foot vessel, put into service in 1958, was well-equipped with lifesaving devices and emergency electronic equipment, according to *The Wreck of the Edmund Fitzgerald* by Frederick Stonehouse. It also carried eighty-three life preservers, two fifty-man lifeboats, and other safety devices.

The weather was calm the morning she departed on a routine trip from Superior, Wisconsin, for Detroit. Two hours into the journey, the *Fitzgerald* caught sight of the SS *Arthur M. Anderson* on its way to Gary, Indiana, and as commonly practiced, the two vessels buddied up for the crossing. The storm intensified. By 7:00 p.m., the National Weather Service had posted gale warnings. Thus began the final hours of the twenty-nine men aboard The *Fitz.*

In its early hours, the storm had caused minor damage to the ship's cargo hatches, according to the History Channel's *Deep Sea Detectives: Death of the Edmund Fitzgerald.* The *Fitzgerald's* Captain Ernest McSorley, a longtime veteran of the Great Lakes maritime industry, did not consider the damage a serious issue. As the two ships progressed eastward and weather conditions deteriorated, Captain McSorley and the *Anderson's* captain, Jesse Cooper, agreed to adjust their course to follow a safer northeast route taking them near Caribou Island, thirty-five miles off Whitefish Point. Gourley reports the *Anderson* was about seventeen miles ahead of

The SS *Edmund Fitzgerald* traverses the St. Mary's River. The *Fitz* was the most modern and largest ship serving the Great Lakes when it sank in Lake Superior on November 1, 1975.

the *Fitz* on the afternoon of November 10. Captains McSorley and Cooper maintained radio communication.

Because the *Fitzgerald* had lost radar capabilities, the crew of the *Anderson* did their best to provide navigational aid to its buddy ship. The History Channel documentary theorizes the *Fitzgerald* may have drifted too close to Caribou Island and unknowingly hit the isle's shallow shoals, causing undetected damage.

Just before 7:30 p.m., Captain Cooper went to the *Anderson*'s pilot house. Records indicate the first mate reported he had just spoken to Captain McSorley, who'd told the sailor they were "holding their own."

Gourley writes that although the *Anderson*'s radar reflected rough sea activity, masking the *Fitzgerald*'s movement, Captain

Cooper knew The *Fitz* was within nine miles of his ship. "For a few minutes he could not see the *Fitzgerald* because a snow flurry restricted his visibility. That was just a few minutes. Then the snow lifted. Cooper could see for 20 miles. There was no *Fitzgerald.*"

Cooper contacted the Coast Guard at Sault Ste. Marie. Their response was disbelief. It seemed utterly impossible that the "Queen of the Great Lakes" could vanish without making a single distress signal. After a second call by Captain Cooper, the Coast Guard rallied a search and rescue mission. Though the wreck site was located three days later, not a sole survivor was found. The mission continued for several weeks but recovered only a few pieces of flotsam from the mighty carrier.

Whatever happened to the *Fitzgerald* occurred so suddenly the crew had no time to put on lifejackets or launch lifeboats. Thousands of pages of Coast Guard documents and numerous dives to the wreck site, including one by Jean-Michel Cousteau and the *Calypso* team, have failed to provide consensus as to what sank the *Edmund Fitzgerald.* Did the damaged hatches allow it to take on too much water during the storm? Did possible hull damage occurring at Caribou Island lead to its demise? Did overload contribute to its fate? Or was it the victim of mysterious forces encompassing the Great Lakes Triangle?

Summer 2010 brought the Discovery Channel's *Ghost Lab* crew to Whitefish Point to conduct a scientific investigation of paranormal activity in the Lake Superior region—the very region that claimed the *Fitzgerald* and two hundred other ships over the years. According to the Great Lakes Shipwreck Museum, which provided support to the mission, the *Ghost Lab* crew reported that

Whitefish Point was one of the most active paranormal sites they had encountered.

What force or forces could cause dozens of ships and aircrafts deemed sea- or airworthy and staffed with qualified captains and crew to experience sudden, complete devastation?

So many incidents occur in the Great Lakes skies that the Federal Aviation Administration established a Lake Reporting Service to automatically initiate search and rescue missions if a flight goes for more than a few minutes without communication with air traffic controllers.

No effort may have been capable of saving the men and women onboard Northwest Flight 2501 when it disappeared on June 23, 1950, over Lake Michigan between St. Joseph and South Haven. In the worst aviation disaster of the period, its crew and fifty-five passengers vanished inexplicably from the air and were never heard from again. The DC-4 plane was westbound out of New York City's La Guardia Airport bound for Seattle, Washington. Captain Robert Lind's last radio communication was a request to fly lower to avoid "other traffic." His request was denied, but Lind defied instructions. It was never clear what traffic in the area the captain wanted to avoid.

By sunrise, the most extensive Great Lakes search ever launched was underway for the missing aircraft using the best technology of the day. Over the next week, debris and human remains washed ashore, closing public beaches. Official investigations into the cause failed to offer an explanation.

Gourley quoted the Civil Aeronautics board report: "None of the radio communications from the flight, including the last, contained any mention of trouble. At the same time, the possibility that this accident resulted from some mechanical failure seems remote. . . ." In 2004, a modern search for the aircraft was launched by a Holland nonprofit group and best-selling novelist and marine archaeologist, Clive Cussler. Using the latest available equipment, the search was resumed each summer until the unsuccessful effort was finally ended in 2010.

The summer of 2010 also marked tragedy for the town of Alma when four prominent residents died in an unexplained air accident over Lake Michigan. It occurred during a medical mission. The pilot of the Cessna craft was the sole survivor. The National Transportation Safety Board's preliminary report found no cause for the fatal crash. It states: "All instrument readings were within normal limits as they crossed the shore near Ludington, Michigan. The head winds were about forty knots 'directly on the nose.' About mid-point over the lake, the engine began to misfire and lose power, with the fuel dropping to about eleven gph. The pilot attempted to regain power by pushing the mixture control to full rich but without effect. He contacted the Minneapolis Air Route Traffic Control and reported that the airplane was losing power, and he switched fuel tanks and adjusted the mixture control in and out to try to regain power. He reported that he turned on the high boost pump and got a short burst of power for about 35 to 40 seconds, but then the engine 'failed completely.'"

The Cessna was located by the Michigan State Police Dive Team on August 1, 2010, in 173 feet of water about five miles off the Ludington shoreline. Two days following the incident, *The*

Morning Sun newspaper reported that passenger Dr. James Hall had scribbled a note to family and friends minutes before the plane dove into the lake. It was later recovered in the doctor's medical bag. "Dear All, We love you. We lost power over the middle (of) Lake Michigan and turning back. We are praying to God that (all) will be taken care of. We love you. Jim." His poignant last words likely echo the final thoughts of the hundreds of souls succumbing to disaster over the Great Lakes.

While these incidents represent some of the best-known events, sudden disappearances within the region occur with a striking regularity. Time and again, official investigations conclude that these incidents are "unexplainable."

Some attribute the great number of accidents to the Great Lakes' brutal storms, and severe weather is undoubtedly the basis for many sea and air accidents. Between 1878 and 1898, the peak of Great Lakes sailing, the United States Commissioner of Navigation reported that 5,999 vessels had wrecked on the Great Lakes. The US Environmental Protection Agency Great Lakes division warns of navigational problems caused by Erie's shallow depths, Superior's rocky coastline and cold temperatures, and Lake Michigan's tricky wind shifts.

Mother Nature throws into the dangerous mix a particularly wicked phenomenon: the *seiche*. A large Great Lakes seiche wave has the potential to wipe ships from the face of an inland sea in the blink of an eye. Seiches are triggered by atmospheric disturbances, shifting winds, or pressure drops, all causing an effect similar to water sloshing back and forth in a bathtub. A single giant seiche wave can arrive completely unannounced on land or sea.

On July 4, 1929, a storm over Lake Michigan produced monster twenty-foot seiche waves. When these waves hit the Grand Haven coast, it entirely engulfed the pier, taking the lives of ten people. Fatal incidents have since been reported at the Holland State Park Beach and at the Lake Michigan basin near Chicago. In 1995, a large Lake Superior seiche caused water to suddenly retreat, dropping water levels three feet in a matter of minutes at Marquette and Point Iroquois. Docked boats were left dangling from moor lines.

Historic reports also tell tales of sudden intense winds occurring on the Great Lakes. Gourley writes that in 1899, the schooner *Hunter Savidge* was crossing Lake Huron heading for Alpena when, without warning, "a wind drove the bow of the ship beneath the surface." The ten-second blast ripped the ship apart, taking five lives. A similar fate reportedly occurred to the schooner *Jamaica* in 1872.

Unexplained incidents in the skies over the Great Lakes account for further mysteries. Planes suddenly disappear from radar, crash, and vanish without a single distress call. In many cases, as in the 2010 Ludington crash, accident investigators find no instrument defect or reason for engine failure. So sudden does the danger arise, pilots fail to eject. Such was the case in the crash of a twin-engine Piper PA-23 in 1964, near the Howell Airport. Minutes after a textbook takeoff, at an elevation of between three hundred and six hundred feet, one engine reportedly misfired while the other engine speeded. With landing gear down, the plane went into a nosedive and crashed. According to Gourley, the official investigation found no probable cause for the fatal accident.

Some attribute mysterious aircraft incidents to the earth's magnetic field's ability to distort instrumentation and technology. Of the six major iron ranges in the United States, three are found in Michigan. These ranges, which stretch across the Great Lakes region, present a plausible explanation for some of the disproportionate number of baffling air accidents.

Others claim UFOs are responsible for the high number of unsolved shipwrecks and plane crashes. Could the "other traffic" the pilot of Northwest Flight 2501 attempted to avoid have been an unidentified flying object invisible to air traffic controllers? In his book *Aliens from Space,* naval aviator Marine Major Donald Keyhoe recounts the events of one of the most famous UFO/aircraft sightings ever recorded. The incident took place on the evening of November 23, 1953. Air Defense Command at the now decommissioned Kinross Air Force Base near Sault Ste. Marie identified on radar an unusual target over southeast Lake Superior. In response, an F-89C Scorpion jet assigned to the 433rd Fighter Interceptor Squadron and piloted by Lieutenant Felix Moncla was scrambled from Kinross. His mission was to check on the unidentified target flying near restricted air space over the Soo Locks. Moving at five hundred miles per hour, Moncla and the onboard radar observer, Lieutenant R. R. Wilson, closed in on the object at about eight thousand feet. Ground controllers watched as the two images on the radar screen drew closer to each other, then merged, then completely disappeared about seventy miles off Keweenaw Point. United States and Canadian search and rescue teams were immediately summoned into action. The search continued for days, but no trace of the plane or men was found.

Keyhoe writes that the Air Force later gave family members conflicting incident accounts. They were told the pilot likely experienced vertigo, causing him to nosedive into the water. They were also told the F-89 collided with a Canadian plane, which Canadian officials repudiated.

The story remained unexplained until 2006, when members of the Great Lakes Dive Company claimed to have located the plane lying upright on the lake bed with the port side missing and the mysterious object it supposedly collided with nearby. Not long after releasing what the company claimed were sonar images of the wreck, experts suggested the images were phony, and the Great Lakes Dive Company vanished as quietly and completely as the men of the Scorpion. The true account of the plane's odd disappearance remains to be discovered.

From giant sturgeons to aliens and time warps, explanations for the inexplicable air and sea disasters within the region are strange by anyone's standards. Many shipwrecks are forgotten over time; others, like the *Rouse Simmons,* grab hold of our imaginations, their legends enduring for decades.

It was almost six decades after the Christmas Tree Ship vanished that she was found lying at the bottom of Lake Michigan. According to a document published by the US National Archives and Reports, diver Gordon Kent Bellrichard stumbled upon the Christmas Tree ship's grave in 1971. He found Captain Santa's well-preserved schooner lying in coastal waters off Two Rivers, Wisconsin, 172 feet below the surface. A 2006 underwater archeological expedition found evidence that the Christmas Tree Ship had nosedived into the sea. However, the exact cause of its demise was not determined, leaving ample room for the mystery to grow. After the Christmas Tree ship disappeared, it was rumored rats living onboard fled the ship before it departed from Thompson Harbor for its deadly voyage, suggesting premonition of disaster. Some say Captain Santa still calls from beyond the grave, while visitors to his wife Barbara's burial site at Chicago's Acacia Park Cemetery claim the scent of evergreen infuses the air surrounding her grave.

Whether one thinks mysterious forces, human error, or Mother Nature's fury account for these baffling fatal events, it is clear that the wild, vast, beautiful Great Lakes region remains a formidable foe for air and sea travelers.

CHAPTER 5

Paul Bunyan: Folklore or Fakelore?

Weary from a long day of timbering in the north woods, a group of shanty boys sat around a camp stove to warm their aching bones. In the shadows of the fire's soft glow, they began to spin outrageous tales to fill the empty hours—stories like the fantastical origins of the Muskegon River.

One spring, Michigan rains fell so hard and fast over the barely thawed ground that Houghton Lake began to overflow its banks. "So Paul took Babe the blue ox and plowed a furrow from the lake down to Lake Michigan. He didn't dare wait until daylight because it was raining so hard. Having to plow the furrow at night in black darkness, he couldn't see so good, and that is why the Muskegon River is so crooked."

Born of the lumber camps, escapades of the great oversized lumberjack Paul Bunyan and his sidekick Babe have been told and retold for generations. How big was the logging giant? Legend tells it took five storks to deliver him as a baby. Like the story of how the Muskegon River was formed, published by E. C. Beck, Paul Bunyan tales capture the imagination with their mix of truth, fiction, and humor.

In his book, *They Knew Paul Bunyan,* Beck retells stories from the winter of the blue snow when Babe, the eleven-foot high ox with a space of "two axe handles and a thumb between the eyes," became forever blue. Beck wrote it was also the season Paul carved the first Great Lakes ship canal. "It was so cold that it froze the flames in the lamps, and we couldn't blow them out. So we just broke off the flames and threw them out the window." According to the tale, when spring came the flames thawed and sparked a fire, burning the St. Mary's River in two. With Lake Superior navigation held up, folks in Duluth begged Paul to take action. "The next morning Old Paul took one of the wagon boxes off a wagon and a shovel and went up there and put that wagon box in where the river burned in two. That was the first ship canal at the Soo. It was quite a job and Old Paul was eighteen minutes late for dinner."

Arising from the "army of the pines," the Mackinaw-wearing supersized folk hero embodied the spirit of the thousands of lumberjacks who drove Michigan's "Green Gold Rush." From the 1860s on, whatever shape the tall tales took, the mighty Paul was always an unequaled hero who tamed the wilderness with Hercules-like strength while showing fairness and kindness to his fellow man. Over time, Paul developed into an iconic symbol for the working man of the period, those brave souls who carved the wilderness with few tools other than their bare hands and strong backs.

If anyone needed a superhero, it was the sturdy souls who spent November through May fighting the forces of nature to harvest Michigan's white pine. The towering evergreens were needed to build the Midwest's great cities and hurriedly rebuild those destroyed by fire. Wooden houses as well as commercial and industrial buildings of the day were extremely vulnerable to flames. It was not uncommon for cities large and small to be consumed by a single blaze. Chicago's entire central business district burned in the fall of 1871.

As a result, construction flourished, and virgin pine standing a straight 80 to 120 feet tall was in high demand. Lightweight, they were easier than other species to send downriver to the hundreds of mills. In his book, *Paul Bunyan: How a Terrible Timber Feller Became a Legend,* award-winning journalist D. Laurence Rogers noted that in 1888, over four billion board feet were cut at Saginaw Valley mills alone, "enough to make a sidewalk of two inch planks, four feet wide that would reach around the earth almost four times."

During the boom, Michigan's green gold outperformed the California Gold Rush. Rogers reported that between 1848 and 1898, Michigan's lumber industry garnered $4 billion. During the same period, the California Gold Rush generated $3 billion.

The forty years in which lumbering was at its peak produced a band of lumber barons who strutted their wealth in Detroit, Saginaw, Bay City, Muskegon, and other river cities. The Manistee Convention and Visitors Bureau claims that during the 1880s boom, Manistee had more millionaires per capita than anywhere else in the United States.

David Whitney was one of the more illustrious lumber kings. "David Whitney proved he could strip the lumber from a hillside without leaving his richly appointed paneled office," reported the

Detroit News. The Detroit multimillionaire invested heavily in properties along Woodward Avenue, once Michigan's most prestigious address, and gained the nickname "Mr. Woodward Avenue." His 21,000-square-foot mansion on the avenue had 52 rooms, 10 bathrooms, 218 windows, 20 fireplaces, and a secret vault.

Fabulous fortunes made by the lumber barons grew at the hands and sweat of the lumberjacks, commonly called shanty boys for the roughly constructed shacks that served as their homes. During the boom years, up to forty thousand shanty boys were employed in Michigan's massive timber harvest, each earning about $1 per day. The poorly paid timber fellers were a microcosm of the American melting pot, a mix of Americans, Canadians, French, Germans, Finns, Welsh, Swedes, Irish, English, Poles, and Native Americans who went by colorful names like Tanbark Bill, Cedar Root Charley, and Slabwood Johnson.

Exaggerated and humorous Paul Bunyan tales distracted timber fellers from their difficult life. Hardships began for them the minute they abandoned civilization for the forests. "The picture presented in that train load of men going into the woods, was a laughably strange combination of the drunkenly sublime and ridiculous," wrote John Fitzmaurice in his book *The Shanty Boy.*

Camp destinations were often remote. Sometimes carrying supplies thirty-five miles, the timber fellers' first order of business was to locate a site near a good water source, then put up temporary shelters of pine boughs, wrote Fitzmaurice. A camp was generally made up of an office, the cooking and eating camp, the bunk camp, a barn and stable, and a blacksmith shop for building sleighs to move felled trees through the snowy woods. In less than two weeks, the camp was usually ready to launch operations and so were the loggers.

Pressure from management to produce was intense. The lumber barons had one mission: cut and get out. This dictated the harvesting of one hundred trees a day. The men achieved this goal working in a gang consisting of two fellers, a butter, two buckers, two skidders, and a team of horses or oxen. The men performed their back-breaking tasks in harsh weather conditions and in isolation.

While luxuries were scarce, food was generally ample. The camp cook made sure the boys ate well. In one week, the crew could put away six barrels of flour, more than two barrels of beef and two barrels of pork, eight bushels of potatoes, and great quantities of butter, vegetables, dried fruits, and dried meats. Thanks to their skill at the stove, camp cooks became heroes in their own right.

"A camp cook feared no man, for the simple reason that all men feared the camp cook," wrote cook Joe Muffreau in a letter published in Beck's book. "Make no mistake, my friends. Every lumberjack knew who buttered his bread; therefore, the cook had nothing to fear from any man, big or small. I was supreme in my cook shack."

During the long evenings, shanty boys entertained each other with one whopper of a story after another, slowly evolving the Paul Bunyan legend. Rogers maintains that the legend grew from a real-life lumber boss, the French Canadian Fabian "Joe" Fournier, who worked in Saginaw pine country. Fondly dubbed "Saginaw Joe," Fournier was a large man with massive hands and a double row of teeth he was known to use to bite off hunks of wooden bar rails.

"He could handle a double-bit axe or his end of a crosscut saw, and as the loggers used to say, make the pines whimper," wrote Rogers.

The name Paul Bunyan is thought to have been derived from Bon Jean, the French Canadian hero of the Papineau Rebellion, according to Rogers. Rogers believes the French pronunciation (bone yaahn) gradually evolved to Bunyan.

The name, the man, and the legend were fused in the public's mind after Saginaw Joe's dramatic demise. The logger and brawler was murdered one November night in 1875, along the Third Street Dock in Bay City. The alleged murderer was a stone mason named Blinky Robertson. If not for Blinky's publicized trial and his controversial acquittal, the Paul Bunyan legend may have faded away along with the lumberjacks.

Joe's murder occurred in a seedy district known to attract shanty boys keen on wild behavior. Brawls and beatings were common during the logging era in the rowdy districts of Bay City and Michigan's other infamous river towns, such as Ludington, Manistee, Saginaw, Muskegon, Cheboygan, and Alpena. These rough towns eagerly drained the corps of shanty boys of their hard-earned winter's pay. It is said that five thousand loggers descended upon Bay City's gaslight saloons and "sin resorts" each spring. Many of the vice dens, hotels, and gambling joints in the river towns were owned by the same lumber barons that employed and exploited the shanty boys at the camps.

After a winter of depravation, shanty boys flocked to town with a pocket full of cash, ready to cut loose like nobody's business. It was their custom, borrowed from the French Canadians, to tie a red sash around their waists to fancy their outfits. As a result, townsfolk called the invading loggers the Red Sash Brigade. Some say the scenes played and replayed in Michigan's river towns made the Wild West look tame. Loggers dropped their money at racy vaudeville-like shows, dog and cock fights, buggy races, and rowing regattas. Prostitution was rampant, with Saginaw and Bay City's houses of ill repute alone employing 1,400 prostitutes. Roscommon, with its reputation as the roughest town in the nation at the time, had only thirty-six buildings. Thirty-four of them were bars, according to Rogers. So when the brawling Saginaw Joe ended up dead, it should have been little surprise to anyone.

Saginaw and Bay City newspaper headlines flashed reports of the logger's murder, and the public closely followed its developments. It seems Blinky escaped capture the night of the crime, although four others implicated in Joe's death were arrested. Witnesses claimed Blinky hit Saginaw Joe in the head from behind with a mallet. A $300 reward was posted for his apprehension. He was eventually located in Saginaw and arrested.

The impending Christmas holidays led to the postponement of Blinky's trial until January. As the trial date neared, public sentiment grew in the stone mason's favor. Thanks at least in part to Blinky's cronies, who advocated for the alleged criminal, Saginaw Joe's rowdy reputation tarnished his victim status. Original witnesses to the crime changed their tunes when placed on the jury stand. Given the benefit of the doubt by the jury, Blinky walked a free man following a rather frenzied three-day trial.

The sensational trial fed Saginaw Joe's legend as a rough and tumble guy. Despite his brawling ways, he was a highly skilled woodsman and considered a top-notch lumber camp boss by the shanty boys. Cold, dark winter nights at camps provided a rich setting for legends to gain steam, and soon tales of Saginaw Joe merged with those of other great timber fellers into a single character, Paul Bunyan.

Those who could spin a story held a special place at camp, and the best storytellers often gained celebrity. Fitzmaurice recounts a hospital agent, George Starrs, who regularly visited timber fellers across the region. "Starrs is a born mimic. A good comic singer and dancer, and as a story teller is simply inimitable. These are the social requisites for a Saturday night in camp, and frequently fun grows so fast and furious that all restraint is cast aside and free license given to every description of monkey-shine and rough horse play."

Irishman Jimmy Conn was another popular Northwoods tale teller, as was the Upper Peninsula logger Matt Surrell of Newberry. This colorful woodland legacy was later adapted into written stories by James MacGillivray, who grew up in Oscoda hearing the tall tales from some of the best story spinners around. MacGillivray worked a number of jobs, ranging from a Great Lakes cargo shipment broker to a prospector and newsman, gaining employment in California, Alaska, Idaho, and Nevada. His star rose after he returned to his Oscoda-AuSable home. In 1906, MacGillivray was working as a news reporter for the local paper when he penned a Paul Bunyan story, *Round River.* The story was published in the paper on August 10, becoming the first Paul Bunyan tale in print.

MacGillivray joined the *Detroit News* staff in 1907. On a slow news day, he expanded his original story, renaming it "The Round River Drive." It appeared in the Sunday News section of the paper, accompanied by an animated sketch of timber fellers gathered around a campfire listening to a companion sharing the outlandish story of how the hero of the shanty boys conquered the challenges of their trade.

In 1912, MacGillivray collaborated with poet Douglas Malloch to pen a poem, "The Round River Drive." Malloch had gained a reputation as the Lumberman Poet. Their collaborative piece was printed in the *American Lumberman* magazine, for which the poet was a columnist. Paul Bunyan was becoming a household name.

Kay Houston wrote of MacGillivray's lumberjack tales in a 1996 *Detroit News* article: "Scholars and writers were attracted to the robust humor of the loggers and in a short time the story of Paul Bunyan became a national saga."

Houston also reported that MacGillivray went on to work for the state conservation office, giving presentations on conservation and fire prevention using photos and film he created. It seemed the Paul Bunyan legend had a life of its own.

William Laughead, an advertising manager for the Red River Lumber Company and an amateur artist, provided the fabled logger with a broad national platform. A former lumberjack, Laughead capitalized on Paul Bunyan's rugged character for a company advertising campaign in 1914, capturing the attention of an ever wider audience. His graphic image of the larger-than-life lumberman was the first Paul Bunyan visual. Laughead's Paul Bunyan sported a thick moustache, cap, plaid Mackinaw jacket, and the infamous red sash.

Laughead went on to develop a series of pamphlets featuring the woodland hero to promote Red River Lumber Company products and services. In 1922, the company published Laughead's first

Oscoda's statue of the supersized lumberjack Paul Bunyan stands guard at Furtaw Field. Oscoda was declared Paul Bunyan's official birthplace in 2005 by the Michigan Legislature.

written piece, *The Marvelous Exploits of Paul Bunyan.* The artist/ writer's work made the legendary giant a true celebrity.

James Stevens, a public relations representative for the forest industry and an author, also published a book of Paul Bunyan tales during this period. His 1925 work based on the oral traditions wove the stories into yarns he believed reflected the admirable character of the hero lumberman. When his work was criticized for not representing authentic tales of the lumber camp, Stevens invested a year interviewing aging shanty boys and mining their memories for story gems. In 1932, he published his second title about the mythical logger, *The Saginaw Paul Bunyan.*

To Stevens's dismay, the book was criticized by academics. "Fakelore!" decried Richard Dorson, a cultural purist. Between 1944 and 1957, Dorson taught at Michigan State University. Dorson had earned his doctorate degree at Harvard University and later founded the Indiana University Folklore Institute, where he concluded his career. Dorson is often cited as the father of American folklore for his study of the links between folklore and culture. In his estimation, Paul Bunyan stories are merely *fakelore,* a term he coined. Fakelore, according to the academic, is the misrepresentation of the oral traditions of historical and ethnic communities. Pure folklore is a myth or legend shared by a particular group and embodying that group's beliefs and values. Dorson thought Paul Bunyan books fell far short of that criteria.

Children's books are the greatest perpetrators of fakelore, according to another academic, Eliot Singer. Singer claims: "The pretense that children's folktale books are folktales is not innocent, not simply a loose, colloquial usage of a technical term. The appeal of these books rests precisely on their alleged representation of folk traditions, on their providing a link to ethnic heritages, on their enabling children to visit other cultures."

Despite criticism by folklore purists, Paul Bunyan books grew in popularity and the myth became more deeply embedded into American hearts, minds, and culture. The lumberjack earned his place among the country's other larger-than-life characters—Pecos Bill, John Henry, and Mike Fink. But some maintain that Paul Bunyan stands taller than all mythical American characters in ways other than stature. Pulitzer Prize–winning American poets Robert Frost and Carl Sandburg immortalized the lumberjack in poem and prose. Sandburg wrote, "Who made Paul Bunyan, who gave him birth as a myth, who joked him into life as the Master Lumberjack, who fashioned him forth as an apparition easing the hours of men amid axes and trees, saw and lumber? The people, the bookless people, they made Paul and had him alive long before he got into books for those who read."

It was this beloved legend coming alive on the pages of a book that gave momentary relief to American troops during World War II. Paul Bunyan's wild tales of mastering the impossible offered courage and solace to soldiers facing their own extreme hardships and dangers. *Paul Bunyan* by Stevens sold 140,000 copies through military exchanges during the war years, according to Rogers.

Over the years, many states, from Maine to California, have professed Paul Bunyan as one of their own, but only Oscoda, Michigan, has the official right to do so. In 2005, the Michigan Legislature passed a resolution declaring Oscoda as the giant logger's hometown. The state document reads: "The legend of Paul Bunyan has endured the test of time. Many current and former logging towns across the United States now claim to be the home of Paul Bunyan; now therefore be it resolved by the House of Representatives that Oscoda, Michigan is recognized as the true birthplace of the legend of Paul Bunyan as first set in ink by James MacGillivray based on the life of logger Fabian Fournier." This resolution was presented to the Library of Congress, the Library of Michigan, and the Michigan Historical Archives.

One year after the resolution was adopted, Governor Jennifer Granholm proclaimed August 10, 2006, as Paul Bunyan Day in Michigan to honor the one-hundredth anniversary of the printing of James MacGillivray's story in the *Oscoda Press*. The governor's resolution states, "The story of Paul Bunyan, richly rooted in Michigan history and tradition, is now considered to be one of America's greatest folk tales."

While Oscoda holds claim to the mythical logger's birthplace, towns across the state honor the fabled giant and his blue ox. Outdoor statues of Paul Bunyan are found not only in Oscoda but also in Ossineke, Manistique, St. Ignace, Alpena, and West Branch.

Folkhero or fakehero, Paul Bunyan's role as the working man's superhero serves the important purpose of providing inspiration and comic relief while continuing to remind us of the mighty deeds Michiganders are capable of accomplishing.

CHAPTER 6

The Ghost Lights of Paulding and Evart

A dozen people huddle beside an old Upper Peninsula road, wrapping their arms tightly around their chests to fend off the chilly evening air. The dusty country thoroughfare was once part of a military road authorized by Abraham Lincoln during the Civil War to prepare for a potential British strike coming from Canada. Today, the historic road leads to what some say is a paranormal phenomenon.

The evening's group of tourists and area residents perch on a hill overlooking a power transmission line stretching through the valley before them. This remote site near the old sawmill village of Paulding, not far from the Wisconsin border, is surrounded by the Ottawa National Forest's nearly one million acres of woods, lakes, rivers, and waterfalls.

As darkness descends, the crowd shivers. They chat in hushed voices, waiting and watching. "There it is!" a stunned voice whispers. Others gasp. What is known as the Paulding mystery light slowly rises out of the valley. The shining orb hovers in the air for twenty minutes. Sometimes it draws close to the group, making the children in the crowd cry with fright. It retreats and comes forth again, morphing from a starlight appearance to a spark and to a glowing ember. After a brief dance across the forest opening, the orb vanishes into the night. Onlookers exchange a few comments before retreating to the safety of their cars and driving away.

Known as the Paulding Lights, these ghostly orbs have mystified the young and old, educated and uneducated, for decades. A few old-timers claim the lights first appeared at the turn of the century, but it was in the 1960s that the lights gained notoriety. The unexplained phenomenon continues to draw large audiences, and most are not disappointed by the performance. For their part, the lights show up almost nightly year-round, making themselves a major point of interest.

An entry in *Weird Michigan: Your Travel Guide to Michigan's Local Legends and Best Kept Secrets* describes one individual's Paulding Light experience. William Kingsley shared his observation, saying, "The light appeared to move, it flickered and swayed as it moved. Its light was reflected off power lines and my jacket. Once, it appeared to split in two."

So mainstream is the ghost-light mystery that the local chamber of commerce advertises it along with the area's traditional recreational activities. "Hunt, fish, camp, see mystery lights." Even the US Forest Service is onboard with the popularity of the phenomenon. The agency erected a sign at the Paulding Light viewing spot featuring an image of Casper the Friendly Ghost as well as the service's official logo. The sign reads: "Paulding Light. This is the location from which the famous Paulding Light can be observed.

Legend explains its presence as a railroad brakeman's ghost destined to remain forever at the sight of his untimely death. He continually waves his signal lantern as a warning to all who visit. To observe the phenomenon, park along the forest road facing north, the light will appear each evening in the distance along the power line right-of-way."

The viewing site is easily accessed by taking State Highway 45 north from Watersmeet for five miles to Robbins Pond Road (Old 45), where you turn left and drive about one-half mile until you come to the US Forest Service sign.

Regional history appears to be the seed for the legend associated with the lights. According to *Hunt's Guide to Michigan,* Route 45, the federal military road ordered by Lincoln, connected Fort Wilkins and the mining port of Copper Harbor. In earlier times, it was a vital connection through the frozen winter landscape for supplies and mail for Copper Country coming from Wisconsin's Green Bay. This area's prosperous copper mining and logging industries of the 1800s operated worker camps that were fertile breeding grounds for tall tales about miners, loggers, and railroad men. But are the fabled Paulding Lights merely the product of overactive imaginations?

Michigan Technological University (MTU) students set out to get to the bottom of the question during the fall of 2010. MTU is a leading public research university known for developing new technologies and environmental studies. It's situated along the Keweenaw Peninsula about seventy-five miles north of the Paulding Light site. A group of students from the university's chapter of SPIE (International Society for Optical Engineering) led by PhD candidate student Jeremy Bos made several road trips to the sight to investigate the phenomena and prepare a scientific analysis, according to *Michigan Tech News*.

Generations of Paulding Light viewers provided the students with a number of theories to debunk. The legend had floated around for at least fifty years, continually gathering a thicker cloak of mystery. One theory holds that the light is the ghost of a railroad brakeman, the legend perpetuated by the US Forest Service sign. Others claim the light is the spirit of a mail carrier ambushed and killed by Indians more than a century ago. At least one woman believes the lights are a mystical sign or portal for entering the next world. In his book *More Haunted Michigan*, Gerald Hunter claims that some individuals speculate the ghost is that of a jealous lumberjack in love with a railroad engineer's wife. When the engineer confronted the lumberjack about the relationship, the lumberjack killed him. It is believed the lights are the engineer's ghost forever bereaving the woman he lost.

Some confuse the Paulding ghost lights with the northern lights, or aurora borealis. Believers of the Paulding phenomenon are quick to point out this mistaken identity. Northern lights splash the night horizon with pulsating streams of red, blue, and green. They are commonly viewed in the skies above Michigan's Upper Peninsula due to the region's proximity to the North Pole, where the show is seen with the greatest frequency. Northern lights occur when electrically charged particles from the sun move along magnetic fields at high speed toward Earth, where they collide with upper atmospheric particles. Colors are created by particular combinations of gases present in the air when these particles meet.

A US Forest Service sign marks the Paulding Light viewing location perpetuating the local ghost legend.

The MTU students were on a mission to learn exactly what was happening in Paulding that had puzzled so many people for so long. During their first trek to the site, the light appeared on cue for observation. During the students' second visit, they came equipped with a telescope. The university news report explained that when the Paulding Lights were viewed through a telescope, students found the light revealed itself to be car headlights along US 45. Using Internet maps, the students pinned down the headlight locations. They then conducted tests by posting students at both the headlight positions and the viewing points. It allowed them to duplicate the light event to support their car-headlight theory. Use of a spectrograph and atmospheric modeling to measure distortion created by pavement heat further substantiated the students' conclusion that the Paulding Lights are nothing mysterious and are merely vehicle headlights. They also concluded that the occasional colored lights spectators report are generated by the colored lights flashed by police vehicles. The fact that the Paulding Lights started to create a buzz at around the same time the stretch of highway noted by student investigators had been rerouted further suggests the mysterious lights aren't so inexplicable after all, only an optical phenomena stemming from US 45 traffic several miles north of the viewing point.

Despite the students' in-depth study and evaluation, many Paulding Light observers remain unconvinced that what they see is an optical illusion. These stalwarts continue to believe that something more peculiar, shadowy, and otherworldly is going on out there.

Similar ominous thoughts are shared by many residents of the Osceola County town of Evart. Even skeptical visitors to the glowing tombstones at Forest Hill Cemetery are spooked by the strange graveyard light show.

As towns go, Evart is an unlikely candidate for sprouting a paranormal legend. Located in the middle of the Michigan Mitten, this small town of about 1,600 people was carved out of the wilderness as a logging and agriculture community during the 1800s and grew into a manufacturing town, benefiting from the state's vital auto industry. Through decades of economic ups and downs, tourism kept the city on the vacationer's radar, largely due to the area's woodlands and the beautiful Muskegon River. Outdoor recreation opportunities still draw anglers, hunters, and paddlers, and a traditional Fourth of July parade and fireworks are a summer highlight. Along Main Street, you find the public library, a few mom and pop shops, a couple restaurants, a beauty salon, day care, a medical office, and an attorney's office. City hall is just one block down from the shopping district, located in the town's old train depot. It's hard to imagine a more all-American small town.

Out of this slice of Americana arises a long unsolved mystery. Follow the old railroad tracks east of town, turn off on 80th Avenue and continue until you come to the Department of Natural Resources Field Office. From here you can see the historic Forest Hill Cemetery, where strange illuminations have baffled residents for more than 150 years. In the old section of the cemetery, the roots of sprawling trees climb above ground while their massive canopies hide the sunlight, blanketing the air and ground with an uncomfortable dampness. Brush away debris from the oldest of tombstones and you find they date back to the 1870s.

Forest Hill Cemetery is the final resting place for at least one famed Evart native, Joseph Guyton. Guyton was the first American soldier to die on foreign ground in World War I. His funeral is said to have drawn ten thousand mourners.

When the original cemetery became filled, the City of Evart added a new section. The ghostly lights make no distinction, shining on old and new tombstones alike.

In the late 1990s, a local journalist threw all of his investigative skills into unraveling the phenomena of the cemetery lights. Jim Crees, a longtime reporter for the *Osceola Pioneer,* had covered his share of news events over the years, but this was perhaps his most unusual challenge. Crees spent days testing, measuring, observing, and charting angles, only to conclude there was no reasonable explanation for the phosphorescent, shimmering tomb lights. And so the ghost tale prevailed.

In 2010, a television crew from the local CBS affiliate examined the mystery of Forest Hill Cemetery, capturing the lights on film and once again unearthing the legend of the glowing tombstones.

The Evart fable is rooted in the mid- to late 1800s, when Michigan's lumber industry boomed. Railroad expansion was promoted at this time to increase efficiency in moving logs to market, allowing lumber barons to increase their fantastic wealth. Recognizing that the days of traveling by horse and buggy were gone for good, the population demanded improved rail transportation, too. Within this economic and social environment, the Flint and Pere Marquette Railroad expanded service from neighboring Clare County to Evart. Workers employed to construct the connecting line lived at a camp located on the grounds of what is today Forest Hill Cemetery.

After a long, hard day's work, many of the railroad men would head from camp to Evart's saloons to unwind. As can be expected, the drinking got out of control at times. To ensure the men found their way home safely after a night on the town, the camp cook, named Guido, lit lanterns along the rail bed to illuminate the trail back to camp for the crew. Guido's son, Marco, also worked at the site and was among the men who frequented Evart's drinking parlors. One night Guido was lighting lanterns as usual when a brawl broke out among the workers walking back to camp along the trail. During the altercation, Marco fell off the bridge crossing the Muskegon River. Even though he couldn't swim, Guido bravely dove into the water to save his son. Both tragically succumbed to a watery death. Marco's body was recovered a few days later; however, Guido's body was never found.

According to legend, his spirit lingered. Following Guido's death, lights continued to glow along the path at night. Oddly, they disappeared whenever someone approached. Folks said it was Guido's ghost still lighting the way for the railroad crew. Disturbed by the strange ghost lights, rail workers abandoned the camp. Soon afterward, the practical Evart citizens transformed the site into cemetery grounds.

Many who dismiss the idea of ghosts acknowledge the presence of the unexplained lights at Forest Hill Cemetery. Across the globe and across the ages, people have reported similar phenomena. On March 1, 2010, National Geographic Channel premiered the episode *Mystery Lights* in its Paranormal series. The program presented the earthquake light theory as an explanation for the mystery-light phenomenon observed around the world.

According to scientists, moving rock beneath the Earth's surface creates electrical charges. When these electrical charges are released at the Earth's surface, the charge is capable of producing what is sometimes called *earthquake lights*. Earthquake lights reportedly take the form of glowing orbs or ribbons of light that stretch across the sky. They may appear days prior to a quake, during a quake, and after a quake, and they can be seen hundreds of miles away from an earthquake epicenter. Some believe geological stress also produces the mystery-light phenomenon.

In a 1991 article, the *New York Times* explained a theory put forth by Dr. Arch C. Johnston of the Center for Earthquake

Research at Memphis State University. Johnston related the phenomena to the effect of high-energy sound waves transmitted through water. Sound waves compress and extend water, forming minuscule bubbles. Bubbles implode into hydrogen and oxygen atoms and recombine into the water. During this process, light photons are released. In a like manner, seismic activity produces high energy waves that move through rocks and water, producing similar bubbles where water is trapped in rock. Under these circumstances, breaking rock would create the light phenomenon.

In recent years, scientists have acknowledged concentrations of radon in areas producing the mysterious earthquake lights. A group of physicists, including physics Nobel Laureate George Charpak, has developed an earthquake predictor based on detection of radon. According to a US Geological Survey analysis, the Western Upper Peninsula is underlain by volcanic rock. Combined with the permeability of its soils, the area has a moderate to high radon potential, possibly linking the geological structure to its ghost lights.

It may be years before scientists are able to determine whether the Paulding and Evart lights are created from gases released into the atmosphere from seismic activity, a sign from the netherworld, or something more common, like decaying matter. Until scientists unravel that mystery, you'll have to draw your own conclusions.

CHAPTER 7

Who Was the Original Rosie the Riveter?

In 1942, only months after the Imperial Japanese Navy's surprise strike against the American base at Pearl Harbor, Hawaii, an ordinary work day for Rose Will Monroe changed the nation. Monroe dutifully punched in at Ford's Willow Run aircraft factory in Ypsilanti with few expectations. But by the end of her shift that day, the young widow was poised to become an enduring symbol for women's empowerment.

After her husband's untimely death in an auto accident, Rose joined the workforce to support her two children and to answer the call for American women to involve themselves in the World War II defense effort. For the first time, women workers were given the task of operating drill presses, welding tools, and heavy casting machinery—jobs formerly believed only men could handle. Rose operated a riveter, and it proved to be her link to history.

She worked at the Willow Run factory at the moment in time when the federal Office of War Information was ramping up a campaign to recruit women into the workforce to meet war production needs. The war machine needed aircrafts, arsenal, and other items in short order. The campaign was meant to fill the sudden labor shortage caused by the large numbers of men drafted or enlisting in the military. The government promotional campaign was developed with the idea to glorify "womanpower" as the patriotic ideal and to draw women into a new role.

A popular song of the time, "Rosie the Riveter" (recorded by Kay Kyser), was already fueling this movement when Hollywood actor Walter Pidgeon visited the Willow Run factory where Rose worked. Pidgeon was participating in a government film promoting war bonds. Bonds were sold during the war to cover military costs, and citizens were urged to purchase the bonds. War bonds sold for $18.75 each and were expected to be valued at $25 ten years later. They were available at neighborhood grocery stores, movie theatres, and other easy-to-access sites. Patriotic-minded celebrities and politicians alike pushed the sales. Even schoolchildren were encouraged to buy the lower-priced war-bond saving stamps. This Victory War Bond campaign turned out to be so successful that by the end of the war, half the population had purchased bonds, for a total of $185.7 billion. It was a breathtaking accomplishment, given that the median annual income in the country at the time was $2,000.

Upon meeting Rose, Pidgeon's instincts told him that the real-life Rosie the Riveter was the perfect subject for his promotional film. It was a stroke of genius. Before long, the campaign to get women into the workforce was known as "Rosie's call."

Women across the nation enthusiastically responded to the call. According to the Ford Motor Company, by 1943 more than 30 percent of Ford workers in machining and assembly departments were women. With competence and loyalty, women had moved from the kitchen, tied back their hair, and rolled up their sleeves to build Ford jeeps, aircraft, tanks, and artillery.

However, Michigan's manufacturers didn't jump onboard the defense effort as easily as the nation's women. The state's solid manufacturing infrastructure made it the logical location for mass production of defense products. Yet, a frustrating past experience made manufacturers hesitant. Michigan government archives state: "During World War I, they had redone their entire production line to manufacture ordnance. Those government contracts were then canceled when the war ended sooner than expected."

To address manufacturers' concerns, the government formed and funded the Defense Plant Corporation, which provided financial aid for converting factories and guaranteeing profits. The automakers ceased car production in February 1942, to focus entirely on war products. Ford produced chiefly aircraft and Jeeps. Rose Monroe's plant significantly contributed to the nation's production of 300,317 military aircraft during the war years. General Motors manufactured tanks, armored cars, amphibious vehicles, aircraft engines, and propellers. Oldsmobile made artillery shells. Because of this massive effort, Detroit was dubbed the "Arsenal of Democracy." When peace was won, Michigan carmakers could proudly claim they had produced $29 billion worth of war goods, including 12.5 billion rounds of small arms ammunition, 245 million shells, and nearly six million guns.

Despite being glamorized by media, factory work in the 1940s was dangerous work. Large numbers of women were injured, disabled, and even killed. Still, women took their role in the war seriously, and the government's highly effective Rosie campaign was an integral part of the defense effort that sparked the nation. It grew beyond one Rosie to eventually represent three million working women. Rosie the Riveter developed into a symbol for the ideal woman of the era: someone strong, loyal, patriotic, and pretty. Because America's women were expected to relinquish their jobs when men returned from war, campaign propaganda focused on reaching middle-class women with slogans like, "Women in the war . . . we can't win without them," and "With sons at war . . . America needs workers!" and "Be a fighter-backer: you can do a lot."

Beloved American artist Norman Rockwell answered the call with his image of Rosie the Riveter which graced the cover of the *Saturday Evening Post* on May 29, 1943. Rockwell's painting further popularized the war muse. As testament to the enduring Rosie legacy, the piece of art sold in 2002 at Sotheby's for $49.9 million.

Rockwell's real-life Rosie was a nineteen-year-old telephone operator from Arlington, Virginia. She was the only one of the three famed Rosie faces from outside Michigan. Rockwell posed the young woman wearing working blues in front of an American flag and paid her $5 a day for two sittings. The artist took poetic license with the painting, turning the slim-figured woman into a muscular, powerful form. It's been speculated that Rockwell used Michelangelo's Isaiah from the ceiling of the Sistine Chapel as inspiration for the figure. So idealized was the symbolic Rosie that Rockwell added a halo above his Rosie's visor. The *Saturday Evening Post* donated Rockwell's image to the war bond campaign, and it was sent on a nationwide tour along with a number of other wartime art works to boost bond sales.

A second true Michigan Rosie took center stage in the war campaign to rally America's women, but it was years before Geraldine Hoff Doyle of Lansing recognized her iconic role. Doyle's face appeared on the US War Production Coordinating Committee's "We Can Do It" poster, according to an homage for the woman published in the *Lansing State Journal.* The popular poster was created by graphic artist J. Howard Miller in 1942. It featured a muscle-flexing woman wearing a polka-dot bandanna and work shirt. Miller's Rosie image was based on a United Press International photo taken of Geraldine while she worked at a metal-pressing plant near Ann Arbor. Geraldine's employment as a factory Rosie proved a short stint. After only a few weeks, she found less strenuous employment at a soda fountain and book store, but her involvement with the poster followed her to the end of her life.

Originally intended for display for a two-week period, the "We Can Do It" poster endures as a symbol of women's power in the twenty-first century. It wasn't until forty-one years after the poster's release that Geraldine recognized herself as the face of Rosie while perusing the pages of a magazine. After that, she called herself the "We Can Do It Girl" and made public appearances across Michigan to sign posters and remind people of the vital role women served during the war years. Despite the poster's fame, Geraldine never earned a dollar from her involvement with it. She died December 26, 2010, at a hospice in Lansing, believing it was her face that inspired the enduring poster.

Scholar James Kimble questioned Geraldine's role in the poster's creation. According to a *New York Times* report, Kimble discovered a vintage photo snapped by an Acme news service photographer in 1942. The photo identified a young factory worker wearing a bandanna as Naomi Parker Fraley. He noted the location as Alameda Naval Air Station in Oakland, California. It affirmed Fraley's belief that she was the girl behind the famous art. Fraley died in 2018, perhaps the sole woman, or one of several women, whose likeness was transformed into the powerful wartime image.

As time passed, more and more wartime women identified with the Rosie images as the campaign continued to work its way into the mainstream of life. It embodied young and old, including one very familiar face: that of movie star Marilyn Monroe. A 1945 cover of *Yank* magazine features the future star working at a Burbank, California, airplane factory when she was still known as Norma Jean Dougherty.

Like Monroe, millions of women responded to the Rosie call. In 1943 in Detroit alone, 269,000 women were employed in manufacturing, according to *Rosie the Riveter: Women Working on the Homefront in World War II* by Penny Colman. However, women's rise to aid the defense effort left employee gaps in other businesses. Colman writes that because of a shortage of waitresses, one-third of Detroit's restaurants closed by late 1943.

Although the war brought legions of women into the labor force, women were employed long before World War II broke out. The book *The Life and Times of Rosie the Riveter* by Miriam Frank, Marilyn Ziebarth, and Connie Field points out that as women's home crafts, like making cloth and sewing, were industrialized, women and children became the country's first factory workers. In the twentieth century, immigrant and minority women staffed laundries, provided domestic services, and were employed at restaurants and other unskilled low-wage jobs. It took the mass movement created by World War II to place women into higher-paying jobs and to open the door of opportunity.

Colman notes that the government's effort to enlist women in the workforce placed them into countless industries. They worked in shipyards, lumber mills, steel mills, and foundries. In the absence of men, they became farmers, police officers, cab drivers, lawyers, clerical workers, and were employed in other occupations, including the military.

The transition to the workplace was not always easy for America's Rosies. Eighteen million were in the workforce during the war years, and for many, discrimination raised its ugly head. Few women received pay equal to their male counterparts, according to Frank, Ziebarth, and Field. Companies found devious ways to shortchange the new workers. The authors wrote: "General Motors paid women less by substituting categories of 'heavy' and 'light' for those of 'male' and 'female.' In many other plants, women were placed in separate job classifications such as 'helper trainee' instead of 'mechanic learner' and accordingly were paid less. In addition, women were rarely promoted to supervisor status."

Discrimination wasn't limited to wages. Unable to accept women in the workplace, male workers often sexually harassed and mistreated their female coworkers, often making working conditions difficult, if not intolerable. For minority women, who faced the addition challenge of breaking racial barriers, the situation was even more difficult.

"Companies saw women's needs and desires on the job as secondary to men's, so they were not taken seriously or given

Lansing's Geraldine Hoff Doyle is the face of Rosie the Riveter in this iconic 1942 government war poster calling women into the labor force.

much attention. In addition, employers denied women positions of power excluding them from the decision-making process of the company. Women wanted to be treated like the male workers and not given special consideration just because they were women," according to an article from the National Park Service, which honors the nation's Rosies with a monument.

As a result of blatant inequalities, women's membership in unions grew from eight hundred thousand in 1939 to three million in 1945, according to Frank, Ziebarth, and Field. Most unions at the time protected the male workers, so women organized, cooperated with one another, and demonstrated to stop discrimination and improve their situation. They managed to form a Woman's Bureau within the United Autoworkers Union. Joining with other unions and women's groups, they became a force for establishing nondiscriminatory practices in the workplace. In 1945, women lobbied Congress to introduce the Pepper-Morse bill guaranteeing women equal pay for equal work. While this bill failed to pass, the concept of equal pay was established.

Pay was only one issue that the nation's Rosies challenged. Unions staffed by men protected their leadership roles. Some unions were more responsive than others to women's rights, but clauses to limit women's stay at a company to the duration of the war were common, and it was widely viewed that their role in society was to maintain positions for the men coming back from the war. It wasn't until after the war that Ford Motor Company and United Auto Workers union added a nondiscrimination clause into contracts.

Not the least of the working Rosie issues was childcare. Like today, good childcare was hard for working women to find. During the war years, some employers offered on-site childcare in which defense manufacturers recouped the cost from the federal government. Community childcare centers were operated by churches and charities. Frank, Ziebarth, and Field report that the Merrill-Palmer School for early childhood education research operated some mixed-race centers in Detroit. Across the country, federally funded centers provided care for one hundred thousand children, but most were shuttered after the war.

Managing home responsibilities was also a challenge for the new women workers, even more so for those whose husbands were fighting the war. Some women formed co-ops to share tasks and to save time and money.

By the end of the war, millions of women were working, bringing home paychecks, and discovering a new sense of self-esteem. The "you can do anything" message from the government was driven home and women liked it. They found a sense of empowerment, respect, and self-reliance through work. So when the nation's men returned home from war, women found still another conflict on the work front.

The government—which had skillfully lured companies into converting to military production and raised an army of women to produce massive amounts of war goods—had failed to plan for the postwar period. Rosies across the nation were simply hung out to dry. Now, instead of promotions to enlist women in the workforce, government campaigns tried to convince women it was their patriotic duty to return to the kitchen. Frank, Ziebarth, and Field note that when defense production ended, women war workers were laid off at a rate 75 percent higher than men. In Detroit, according to Colman, a survey determined that 72 percent of workers who had been laid off after the war wanted to work but couldn't find jobs. They were simply sent home.

Some women, having won clout within unions, fought back. Others returned to low-wage jobs. A few held on. Following the war, Rose Will Monroe's career consisted of a series of jobs. As a single mother, working wasn't a choice. She learned to drive a cab, operated a beauty shop, and founded Rose Builders, a construction company focused on luxury homes. For many years, she nurtured a dream born of her days at the aircraft factory. More than anything, Rose wanted to become a pilot. She accomplished her goal while in her fifties and then joined her local aeronautics club. Rose died at the age of seventy-seven.

Three years following Rose Will Monroe's death, the National Park Service dedicated the Rosie the Riveter Memorial honoring all of the nation's women war workers. Two hundred real-life Rosies attended the ceremony in Richmond, California, the memorial site.

With unmatched courage and dedication to country, Rose Will Monroe and the army of World War II Rosies changed the world forever. The number of working women in the United States never again fell to pre-war levels. The example set by the millions of Rosie the Riveters was their legacy to the daughters of this country who carry on the fight for equal wages, affordable child care, and freedom from workplace harassment.

CHAPTER 8

Extraterrestrial Visitors

Born in 1951, John Shepherd grew up in northern Michigan during the golden age of television. His young imagination was sparked by science fiction programs like *The Twilight Zone, The Outer Limits,* and *One Step Beyond.* When the young thinker walked beneath the vast, star-filled skies, he wondered what might be out there. These imaginings launched Shepherd's lifelong quest to reveal the secrets of the cosmos. Toward that end, he personally invested thousands of dollars for the development of UFO research technology.

At age twenty, Shepherd formed Earth Station One and Project STRAT (Special Telemetry Research and Tracking) at the Antrim County home where he was raised. One year later, STRAT was officially established as a sole proprietorship and was up and running. Using an ultra-low frequency radio transmitter, Shepherd began broadcasting electronic tone pulses toward the stars. The project grew in scope, eventually spanning twenty-five years of Shepherd's life.

The founding of STRAT coincided with an active period of UFO sightings. One of the most widespread series of reported Michigan sightings began on March 14, 1966, in Washtenaw County. More than one hundred witnesses testified to spotting mysterious flying objects, including William Horn, a civil defense director, four Washtenaw County sheriff deputies, a Dexter patrolman, and many citizens. A 1995 *Detroit News* article recounting the events of a March 17, 1966, sighting by Washtenaw County Sheriff Deputies, Sergeant Neil Schneider and Deputy David Fitzpatrick, noted that the officers observed "three or four red, white and green circular objects oscillating and glowing near Milan about 4 a.m. They called Willow Run Airport officials who could not confirm with radar."

Three days later, two other deputies reported chasing similar objects in northern Washtenaw County. Residents in neighboring Livingston and Monroe counties also reported sighting these unexplained sky objects. That night, a patrolman for the Washtenaw County village of Dexter spotted a UFO featuring red and green flashing lights around 9:30 in the evening. The UFO reportedly paused over a scout car and then disappeared upward, accompanied by a second UFO. The county sheriff ordered six patrol cars and fifteen law officers to the scene. At one point the officers unsuccessfully chased one of the UFOs along Island Lake Road.

Washtenaw County Deputy Sheriff Buford Bushroe was another witness to the mysterious flying machine. The same *Detroit News* article reported Bushroe's observation. "It looked like an arc. It was round. We turned around and started following it through Dexter for five miles. It was headed west and we stopped. We lost it in the trees. Either the lights went off or it took off with a tremendous burst of speed. It was about 1,500 feet above the ground. It moved along at about 100 mph. We were doing 70 before losing it near Wylie Road."

The attention did not deter the UFOs. On March 22, dozens of witnesses again reported seeing a flying object near Dexter and Hillsdale.

By March 29, sightings had been reported over communities across southern Michigan, including those in Macomb and Oakland counties, as well as over the cities of Bad Axe, Flint, and Ann Arbor. April brought reports of sightings in the Upper Peninsula near Marquette. The next year, sightings were reported in Ann Arbor, Grand Rapids, Ypsilanti, and Grand Haven. The Grand Haven sightings were confirmed by local police. By 1968, Selfridge Air Force Base in Harrison Township near Mount Clemens was receiving about three UFO reports weekly.

When the sighting reports first emerged in 1966, a single politician responded to citizen concerns, the late President Gerald Ford. United States Congressman Ford of Grand Rapids was House Minority Leader at the time. In a March 25, 1966, radio broadcast, Ford told constituents, "I believe Congress should thoroughly investigate the rash of reported sightings of unidentified flying objects in southern Michigan and all over the country. I feel a Congressional inquiry would be most worthwhile because the American people are intensely interested in the UFO stories, and some people are alarmed by them."

Ford went on to say, "Air Force investigators have been checking on such reports for years but have come up with nothing very conclusive."

He called for a full-blown investigation and requested the House Committee on the Armed Service or Science and Aeronautics Committee hold public hearings. The Congressman harshly criticized the Air Force's brief investigation of the Michigan sightings by government-appointed astrophysicist J. Allen Hynek of Northwestern University. Hynek dismissed the sightings as swamp gas, pranks, or the effect of planet Venus rising. In a news release, Ford refuted Hynek's claims, including statements from a retired Air Force colonel and a scientist from M.I.T. The news release noted Ford's office had received dozens of telegrams and letters from citizens requesting an investigation.

In a March 30, 1966, radio broadcast, Ford said, "I do think that the American people want a better explanation of UFOs than they have been getting. If my mail is any indication, there are many, many people who find it extremely difficult to believe some of the stories put out by the government on this and other subjects."

Despite Ford's pleas, neither the Armed Services Committee nor the House Science and Aeronautics Committee took public action, but conceded to pressure and held secret meetings. In an April 21, 1966, written statement, Ford responded by saying: "Those who scoff at the idea of a Congressional investigation of UFOs apparently are unaware that the House Armed Services Committee has scheduled a closed-door hearing on the matter Tuesday with the Air Force and that Rep. Joseph E. Karth, D-Minn., headed by a three-man subcommittee which held two days of hush-hush hearings five years ago on behalf of the Science and Astronautics Committee. Karth has confirmed in conversation with a member of my staff that he conducted these secret hearings."

The statement went on to share that subsequent to the secret hearings Karth made a report to the full committee, but nothing was publically released. Ford then demanded the government open up on what they knew about the UFO sightings. Congress bent to Ford's demands by promising to arrange a neutral scientific investigation led by top scientists, although Ford still wanted an open congressional investigation.

The new two-year investigation ordered by the government was directed by Edward Condon. His "Scientific Study of Unidentified Flying Objects," known as the Condon Report and released in 1968, dismissed UFO sightings. Criticized for poor science and called a ruse by some, the report served to end government involvement in the investigation of unidentified flying objects. Other elements influencing the government's decision to drop UFO studies included a review of Air Force UFO investigations dating from 1940 to 1969. During that twenty-nine-year period, the Air Force investigated 12,618 reported sightings. "Of these, 11,917 were found to have been caused by material objects such as balloons, satellites, aircraft; immaterial objects such as lighting, reflections, and other natural phenomena; astronomical objects such as stars, planets, the sun and moon; weather conditions and hoaxes," according to the US Department of Defense. However, 701 sightings remained unexplained.

After Ford was elected president, he seemingly abandoned the effort to get to the bottom of the UFO mystery. According to www .presidentialinfo.com, when pressed for an explanation as to why he dropped the UFO issue, Ford responded: "During my public career in Congress, as vice president and president, I made various requests for information on UFOs. The official authorities always denied the UFO allegations." It was unclear who these "official authorities" to which he referred were or why he, the nation's top official, was not provided the information he supposedly sought.

Despite government's retreat from the UFO issue, one of its lead investigators jumped sides. A consultant hired by the government for more than two decades to debunk UFO sightings became the "Galileo of UFOlogy." J. Allen Hynek, the scientist called to investigate the 1966 UFO sightings in Michigan and who had dismissed them as natural phenomena, also served as a consultant to the United States Air Force's major UFO studies, including Project Blue Book. Although Project Blue Book was shuttered following the Condon Committee report, Hynek continued to study UFOs, publishing several books. We have Hynek to thank for the familiar phrase "close encounters." After years of investigation, the scientist's view of UFOs dramatically shifted from skepticism to embracing the possibility that intelligent life exists. In 1972, he founded the Center for UFO Studies, which continues to operate today.

Meanwhile, back in Michigan, UFOs continued to visit, as reflected by a growing number of eyewitness reports. Shepherd's Project STRAT Earth Station One went into high gear in 1973, when sightings multiplied in the state's northern region. His oscilloscope, in conjunction with the electric power lines, enabled him to measure any unusual electromagnetic activity. During the flurry of sightings, the self-taught techie picked up harmonic interference with his elaborate set-up. As UFO activity increased, he expanded his equipment, which soon encompassed the 1,200-square-foot home where he grew up. A sixteen-foot by thirty-eight-foot addition was constructed to house a two-story, one-thousand-watt, sixty-thousand-volt, deep-space radio transmitter. Combined with other high-power, low-frequency amplifiers, the transmitter enabled Shepherd to send music programs great distances into space. For more than two decades, he transmitted a variety of music from Earth Station One in hopes it would arouse extraterrestrial interest in interacting with humankind. Shepherd broadcast six to eight hours daily until lack of funds forced him to discontinue operations.

The Michigan man's expertise drew widespread attention. Shepherd garnered media attention during the 1980s and 1990s and appeared on several national television programs, including *PM Magazine, Joan Rivers,* and the TBS cable network show *Searching for UFOs.* In 1991, he was the subject of the film, *In Advance of Landing,* a story highlighting the work and passion of extraterrestrial researchers.

Over the years, the numbers of UFO sightings tended to rise and fall. In 1994, another March sighting along the West Michigan coast near Muskegon made headlines. This time, not only were there eyewitnesses, but the object was also verified by radar. The *Grand Rapids Press* reported that an Ottawa County police officer and others spotted flashing red and green lights and cylindrical shaped objects over Lake Michigan south of Holland at about 10:15 p.m. At that same point in time, tower operators at Muskegon County Airport saw what they believed to be aircraft flying in formation. At the same point in time, a National Weather Service worker noticed an object on radar moving at high speeds near South Haven. The news article stated that an investigator from the Mutual UFO Network (MUFON) concluded the speed was within the range of man's ability, but that the object hovered and produced no sound did raise questions.

That same spring, sixteen UFO sightings were reported in the Thumb region. Sightings of triangle-shaped flying objects also came in from Caro, Cass City, and Lake Odessa. The physical description of these objects was similar to what Muskegon area residents had witnessed. *The Grand Rapids Press* reported that the Thumb eyewitnesses described the objects as "triangles with round corners, accented with two red lights and one white light."

Apparently, the great state of Michigan appeals to extraterrestrials of different sorts. On an August day in 2003, a southeast Michigan farmer was driving his combine through his wheat field when he came upon an unexplainable phenomenon: crop circles. According to www.WorldNetDaily.com, the three circles measured fifty-one feet, ten feet, and eight feet in diameter. Investigator Jeffrey Wilson, who earned his graduate degree in physics and chemistry at Eastern Michigan University, told local reporters that holes in the affected plant stalks are an indication that moisture within the plants was heated rapidly, not something a prankster could pull off. Tests also showed the layers of wheat were pressed in opposing swirl formations. According to Wilson, the final proof that the formations were authentic was the colored hourglass shapes found in the wheat. While some crop-circle investigators entertain the idea that the mysterious circles are connected to UFOs, Wilson isn't one of them. The WorldNetDaily.com article noted that in Wilson's investigation of more than 130 crop circles prior to the 2003 event, he found two key links: 90 percent were near transformers attached to power lines and most were within three hundred yards of a body of water. "Wilson told the *Daily Press & Argus* the crop circle phenomenon results from an electrical imbalance. He theorizes irrigation strips ions away from the soil beneath the wheat field, creating a negative electrical charge. Meanwhile, the electricity running through power lines generates a positive electrical charge." Crop circles supposedly happen when the process is triggered by an unknown force. Other investigators of the Livingston County crop circle believed the "mysterious force" could be UFOs.

In 2007, another Michigan farmer had the surprise of his life. Jerry Buglinski was working his field near Owosso in Shiawassee County when he came upon a fifteen-foot crop circle. Over the course of a few weeks, five crops circles appeared in his fields of soy and clover. He told *The Flint Sun Journal* that in forty-five years of farming, he had never seen anything like it, nor had his friends. According to Michigan State University Extension and Shiawassee County Soil Conservation District offices, no other area farms were affected. But the Independent Crop Circle Researchers' Association has documented twenty-six incidents of crop circles in Michigan, beginning with a 1932 incident near Manchester in Washtenaw County. The report noted multiple circles and "balls of light" appearing after the circles were discovered.

Reports of mysterious objects over Michigan fields, cities, forests, and waters continue. The nonprofit Michigan Mutual UFO Network is a chapter of the international organization dedicated to collecting and analyzing UFO data. Between June 1, 2009, and May 31, 2010, its field investigators studied 236 reported UFO

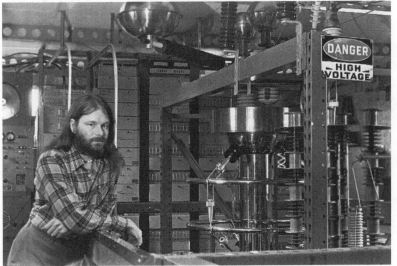

COURTESY OF JOHN SHEPHERD, WWW.PROJECTSTRAT.COM

John Shepherd sends electronic tones into space from his Earth Station One.

sightings in the state, including the following sighting near Okemos in Ingham County near Lansing.

MUFON's case number 21999 contains eyewitness testimony of the February 16, 2010, UFO sighting. At about 3:00 p.m. on that cloudy afternoon, the witness noticed unusual movement at treetop level while driving south on North Meridian Road. Pulling the car to the side of the road, the witness reported seeing a cigar-shaped object about one hundred feet tall and the length of a football field that was about one thousand feet off the ground.

"It was a matted flat charcoal black with very defined edges. It seemed like it was outlined a darker black at the edges. If it were not for the darker edges, it almost would have been camouflaged to the clouds behind it, but the edges made the shape very defined and stand out." The witness pulled off along an overpass to observe the phenomenon. "I was not stopped but maybe thirty seconds and a lightning-like, almost blinding pulse type intensity flash of blue white clear light in the sky at the same height as the object was flying. The flash was not lightning. It held a large oblong shape for the entire time it was visible—about six seconds."

Michigan can claim a long history of UFO reports, but it's not the highest-ranked state for extraterrestrial visits. For example, during the month of January 2011, MUFON reported Michigan had six UFO reports, while California, the highest reporting state, had forty-seven reports. MUFON reported 169 UFO sightings in Michigan in 2017.

MUFON admits that upon investigation the majority of UFO sightings are found to have plausible explanations, but as even the US Air Force determined, an uncomfortable percentage of unexplained incidents keep us asking the same question that young John Shepherd asked: What secrets hide within this vast and mysterious cosmos?

CHAPTER 9

The Underground Railroad's Secret Quilt Code

Every summer in the tiny Wexford County village of Harrietta, folks get together for the Blueberry Festival, a hometown event highlighted by pie-eating contests, an ice cream social, music, a parade, children's games, and a quilt show.

In 2010, the star of the quilt show was a sampler-style design depicting an intricate code believed to be devised in the 1800s. The secret quilt code provided information guiding African-American fugitives to freedom via the Underground Railroad. The show's quilt was the work of a group of fifteen women who call themselves the Harrietta Stitchers.

The Stitchers' project was inspired by a group member who came to the club asking for help in locating secret code patterns. Moved by the historic significance of the quilt code, club members eagerly adopted her idea as a group project. Each member contributed a quilt square representing one step in a slave's escape. In the time-honored tradition, the Harrietta Stitchers sat side by side to sew the quilt together, all the while contemplating this inventive map created in the name of freedom.

Throughout the six-month creative process, the ladies learned much, thought much, and talked much about the secret code said to have directed untold numbers of slaves to freedom through Michigan's Underground Railroad. "We had conversations about the desperation of people trying to get to freedom. The difficulty of being illiterate and not being able to show yourself," said stitcher Mary Morisette.

In this small rural community of less than two hundred people, surrounded by rolling hills and deep forests, the story of America's human exodus to freedom unfolded in their laps, stitch by stitch.

During the days of slavery, the route to freedom available in northern states and Canada was known as the Underground Railroad. Those who sheltered and aided escaping slaves from southern states were called conductors. The clandestine escape network provided the ticket to freedom for an estimated one hundred thousand slaves between 1830 and 1865. Because of its geography and influential abolitionist citizens, Michigan was a prime gateway on the route to freedom, human dignity, and opportunity. But how did illiterate, impoverished slaves lacking transportation find their way from the south through wilderness and past lynch mobs on a journey of hundreds of miles?

In 1999, historian Jacqueline Tobin and art history professor Raymond Dobard, PhD, offered an explanation in their book, *Hidden in Plain View*. The book revealed a secret quilt code, as told to Tobin by an aging African-American quilter named Ozella

McDaniel Williams. Williams explained how slaves used the familiarity of something as ordinary as the household quilt to communicate times and routes for escape. Ten fabric patterns combined with knotting patterns messaged fugitive slaves, telling them when to prepare for escape, what to do, and where to go. Hung from windows or fences, they were ingenious maps, according to Williams, and possibly gave clues to safe houses.

Michigan was the Promised Land for many. From the time it became a territory in 1805, its people supported the antislavery movement, in part because a great number of the state's early settlers came from New England's antislavery movement. By 1810, Michigan was home to 4,618 African Americans, according to census figures. Free African Americans established a thriving community in Detroit, where they found rare opportunities for education.

In addition to Michigan's support of the antislavery movement, because the state is surrounded by the Great Lakes, its geography discouraged slave hunters while its network of lakes and rivers provided a network of easily accessed escape routes.

Influenced by the views and strong leadership of town founders, Ann Arbor and the Washtenaw County communities of Ypsilanti, Dexter, Scio, and Geddesburg served as the seat of the state's antislavery movement. In her book, *The Underground Railroad in Michigan,* Carol Mull highlights the Underground Railroad activities of the founder of the community of Dexter and Dexter Township. "In 1826, Harvard-educated Samuel Dexter was appointed Chief Justice of Washtenaw County in the Territory of Michigan. Judge Dexter's first house on the Huron River and close to the railroad line laid in the late 1830s was open to everyone arriving in the region."

The Underground Railroad network was widely supported in Michigan by religious groups, including Quakers and Wesleyan Methodists, as well as by free slaves. In 1832, Adrian resident Elizabeth Margaret Chandler formed the Logan Female Anti-Slavery Society, giving women an important role in the movement to emancipate slaves and integrate Blacks into American culture. In 1853, the Michigan Anti-Slavery Society was established, providing membership to both men and women.

For the most part, Michigan was the destination for fugitive slaves coming from middle states such as Kentucky and Missouri, where tobacco and hemp were key crops. The oral history offered by Williams, a retired California schoolteacher, reveals that the secret-code quilt was memorized by escaping slaves from a sampler quilt containing ten individual design blocks, each depicting an instruction. Quilts made entirely of one design were then used to communicate each escape step. Because it was an everyday practice to hang quilts from fences or open windows to air, coded quilts did not raise landowners' suspicions.

Williams related that the "Monkey Wrench" quilt pattern signaled the first step in a fugitive's odyssey. It told the slave the time to prepare for the journey was at hand. When the "Wagon Wheel" appeared, it was a sign escape would be via a wagon. The "Bear's Paw" indicated a fugitive was to follow bear tracks north. "Crossroads" directed slaves to Cleveland, Ohio, a major point in the escape network. The "Bow Tie" told fugitives to dress to fit into a community. The "Log Cabin" quilt directed fugitives to draw a cabin in the dirt as a means to identify a conductor or other safe person. The "Shoofly" pattern signaled it was time to scatter. The

A secret-code slave quilt owned by young quilter Danielle Brown is the subject of study by her fourth-grade classmates at Charles Lindberg Elementary in Dearborn.

"North Star" and "Flying Geese" patterns directed fugitives north to Canada, and the "Drunkard's Path" warned the escapee to take a zigzag route, probably meant to confuse slave hunters.

A quilter's knots and ties provided another layer of instruction, according to Wilson. Slave quilt makers typically used twine to hold the batting and quilt top together. Ties were placed several inches apart and tied on the quilt top. The effect on the quilt back was that of a grid. It is thought each tie marks the distance of five or ten miles, the distance a slave on foot could travel in one day.

Michigan abolitionists may have provided fugitives with safe stops, but Canada equated to permanent safety for fugitives. In 1833, slavery was abolished in Canada as a result of the British Imperial Act, which prohibited slavery throughout the empire.

Escaping a slave state was always a treacherous proposition. Any help increased the chances of success. To avoid slave hunters, fugitives often hid in rocks, swamps, or any other place they could find. Underground Railroad safe houses were located about every fifteen miles. Fugitives usually traveled by night and were hid in barns, cellars, or houses by day.

In the 1930s, the Ann Arbor home of William Perry was documented by the Historic Buildings Survey as having a secret hiding place between the walls of a fireplace large enough to shelter several people. Mull's book reported that as late as 2006, a hiding place between cellar stairs and a crawl space was identified in a Saline home. Some homes dating back to the era have been found to have tunnels or false floors to offer safe shelter.

According to historic records, Michigan provided more than two hundred "depots," or safe stops, in the Underground Railroad network along several different pathways to Canada. Lake Huron via Saginaw Bay at Bay City was one of the northernmost outposts. The Great Lakes freedom trail was also accessed from west Michigan ports. From New Buffalo or St. Joseph, fugitives traveled Lake Michigan to Mackinac Straits, then to Lake Huron, and finally to Canada. The Detroit Underground Railroad station, code-named "Midnight," helped fugitives across the Detroit River into Canada. Another Underground Railroad route linked Toledo, Ohio, with Detroit. Another connected Toledo, Ohio, to Adrian, then to Morenci, Tecumseh, Clinton, Saline, Ypsilanti, Plymouth, Swartzburg, River Rouge, and finally, Detroit. The network also included the Grand River Trail from Indiana and Illinois through Michigan's Holland, Grand Rapids and Lansing, to Williamston to Howell to Brighton, to Farmington and then Detroit. Other routes led to Canadian crossings at Sault Ste. Marie and Port Huron.

Mull's book offers a description of one Underground Railroad operation in Detroit. "Agents met at a lodge on Jefferson Avenue where secret meetings were held. They often hid people in the house of J. C. Reynolds, a black worker on the Michigan Central Railway, moving them in the dark one by one. They were fed and provided clothing. 'Our boats were concealed under the docks, and before daylight we would have everyone over. We never lost a man by capture at this point, so careful were we, and we took over as high as 1,600 in one year.'"

Under pressure from southern states, Congress passed the Fugitive Slave Act of 1850, bringing the issue of slavery to a head in the young nation. The federal law allowed for the recapture of fugitive slaves, even in free states, and mandated federal marshals aid in their recapture or face a $1,000 fine. Residents of free states, like Michigan, resented being forced to support slavery. Michigan was among the states adopting legislation to counter the federal rule. In 1855, it passed the Michigan Personal Freedom Acts 162 and 163, providing a level of protection to fugitives.

The compelling story of the secret quilt codes went viral after *Hidden in Plain View* was featured on *The Oprah Winfrey Show* in 1998. In a few short years, the code concept became a widely accepted fact. Despite the popularity of the secret quilt code as a guiding force for freedom, many scholars, quilt historians, and Underground Railroad experts argue that it is nothing more than a fanciful myth. A 2007 *Time* article pointed out that the secret-code quilt theory was based on a single family's oral history and had no other supporting sources. Some experts maintain that certain quilt patterns that have been attributed to the secret quilt codes were not in existence during Underground Railroad days. Previously, a 2004 *National Geographic News* article noted the lack of any mention of quilt codes in nineteenth-century or 1930s oral testimonies of former slaves. And no quilts have survived to corroborate the theory. Without such evidence, most scholars conclude the quilt code is merely legend.

Not so fast, cry quilt code proponents. The fact that quilts did not survive more than one hundred years is hardly surprising. Quilts were made from low-quality textiles, washed with harsh lye soap, and subject to heavy use. Proponents also maintain that the reason the code did not appear in historical narratives is related to who gathered the accounts from slave refugees. Generations of slaves were raised to protect secret communications from slave holders. Without the ability to read or write, perpetuating slave history depended on family oral traditions. Most documentation of the slave era was gathered, compiled, and recorded from the abolitionist point of view.

Tobin and Dobard also support the code theory by making the connection between symbolisms used in African textiles to the slave quilts. They write: "Communicating secrets using ordinary objects is very much a part of African culture in which familiarity provides the perfect cover. Messages can be skillfully passed on through objects that are seen so they often become invisible. These objects are creative expressions of African artisans and give tangible form to the cultural and religious ideas of their kingdoms."

In the presence of this debate, the secret quilt code gained increasing attention. It became the subject of numerous books, articles, and lectures. Quilting books, like those used by the Harrietta Stitchers, became available based on the encoded patterns. Relatives of Ozella McDaniel Williams even developed a cottage industry based upon the code.

Troubled by the unsubstantiated nature of the quilt code, scholars continued to attempt to debunk what they believed was a myth. It has been an uphill battle. Debate was inflamed when a $750,000 statue of escaped slave Frederick Douglass commissioned for New York City featured quilts showing the secret code.

The secret quilt code fails to fall silent. Libraries and museums across Michigan create exhibits featuring quilts of the symbolic blankets in informational exhibits. The legend has made its way into exhibits as diverse as those hosted by Plymouth Historic Museum in Plymouth, which thousands of schoolchildren toured, to rural

Lake County's Luther Area Public Library. The quilt code eventually found its way into the school system as part of the curriculum.

Unbelievers of the code worry that the secret-code quilt theory diminishes the important messages we need to learn from our country's slavery history. On Kate Clifford Larson's website, the historian and biographer of the African-American abolitionist Harriet Tubman expresses her belief that in the end, truth serves children best. She writes:

"I believe that the reason the quilt theory is taught in so many schools is because we as a nation still have a difficult time learning about, remembering, and talking about our slavery past. What better way to teach children about slavery than by dressing the story up all cute and pretty with quilt patterns and kindly folks who used them to guide runaways to freedom—then we don't have to talk about the realities of slavery, and of running away, etc. It seems to me to be part and parcel of the continued erasure of African American history—by creating mythical stories the truth is eventually lost. No one needs myths as a substitute for history, or as a way to explain the complications of history. There is plenty of the real stuff out there, waiting to be exposed and taught to everyone. What we should be teaching adults and children is the truth, and specifically, that slaves didn't use quilt patterns—they used their own wits and bodies to fight their way to freedom."

Still, the idea of a secret code is compelling and holds plausibility for women like the Harrietta Stitchers. "In my mind, there's a great possibility that some of these blocks were used to show slaves ways to prepare for the journey," Morisette said.

When the Stitchers' secret code quilt was raffled at festival, its winner was eight-year-old quilter Danielle Brown. Brown was a fourth grader at Charles Lindbergh Elementary in Dearborn, where the quilt became a study aid during the class unit on the Underground Railroad.

Fiction or fact, the legend of the secret quilt code keeps alive the American slaves' courageous struggle for freedom and the critical role Michiganders assumed in building a country providing "liberty for all."

CHAPTER 10

Lords of the Underworld

Tommy pulled his well-worn jacket tightly around his thin body to fend off the frigid night. Slung across his shoulder was a newspaper satchel, fully half as big as the eight-year-old. "Extra! Extra! Purple Gang members arrested!" he cried as he waved the latest edition of a Detroit newspaper, fighting for the attention of passersby. Newsies like young Tommy brought the latest events to the streets a century before Tweets delivered it to electronic in-boxes. When important happenings occurred, extra editions were printed and hawked along street corners by a corps of children. During the 1920s and 1930s, Detroit's Purple Gang kept the newsies busy.

In the annals of American crime, the Purple Gang ranks among the most savage mobsters of all time. Led by four brothers, the Purple Gang is credited with more than five hundred gangland murders. During their heyday, they fearlessly ruled the Motor City's underworld—controlling Detroit's illegal liquor, gambling, prostitution, and narcotics trades.

The gang was an outgrowth of socioeconomic conditions of the era and the integration of immigrants, or lack of it, into America's mainstream. In the early 1900s, the country absorbed an influx of Italian, Polish, Irish, and Jewish immigrants, who flocked to Detroit in hopes of finding jobs in the developing auto manufacturing industry. But poverty was rampant in the ethnic communities, and rivalries raged.

Abe, Joe, Ray, and "Izzy" Bernstein lived in a Jewish neighborhood on Detroit's lower east side, near Eastern Market (still the state's largest farmers' market). The boys attended Bishop Ungraded School on Winder Street, where they learned to throw their muscle around. Before long, the Bernsteins and several of their school cohorts took their bullying ways to the streets, terrorizing those living and doing business in the Hastings Street area. The youth extorted schoolchildren, rolled drunks for change, and attempted to hustle protection money from street vendors. If vendors failed to fork over cash, the boys destroyed their fruit and vegetable stands.

The wayward teens soon escalated their criminal careers from troublemaker status to ruthless crime czars as Prohibition escalated crime and corruption to a whole new level. Ironically, legislation opened the door. On May 1, 1918, one year before the federal government restricted the sale of alcohol, the state of Michigan adopted legislation making it a dry state. Consequently, Detroit became the first major city in the United States under Prohibition. It was a perfect storm for delinquents like the Bernsteins, who eagerly manipulated the advantage.

The gang worked their way into playing a leading role in Detroit's illegal liquor market, which accounted for $215 million in annual sales, second only to the city's automobile industry. Detroit's geographic location allowed the Detroit River, Lake St. Clair, and the St. Clair River to carry 75 percent of the liquor consumed in the nation during the Prohibition era, according to *The Detroit News*. And the Purple Gang was at the bottom of it all.

The young gangsters found mentors in the mobsters Henry Shorr and Charlie Leiter, who ran Oakland Sugar House at Oakland and Holbrook Avenues, a legitimate business selling brewing supplies. The older men's company was a front for their illegal activity of establishing alley breweries and even complete brewing plants in old barns and warehouses, according to crime expert Paul Kavieff in his book, *Detroit's Infamous Purple Gang*. Working for Shorr and Leiter, the youth became skilled at hijacking and extortion and learned to wield a gun. Once they had some experience under their belts, they were ready for bigger jobs and often served as guards for wealthy gamblers.

As the gang's income grew, they enjoyed flaunting their wealth and made the luxurious Book-Cadillac hotel their gang headquarters. When completed in 1924, the Italian renaissance hotel was the tallest hotel in the world, and from this lavish locale the Purple Gang seized the city's underworld.

The gang embedded themselves in the underworld with their involvement in the 1925 Cleaners and Dyers War. The conflict resulted from an attempt to regulate prices in Detroit's cleaning and dyeing industry by a price-fixing consortium. Once formed, racketeers were called in to strong-arm the city's cleaners and dyers into participation, or face retribution. Those who refused were dealt with by the Purple Gang. Uncooperative cleaners and dyers saw their laundries demolished, their laundry hijacked, and their drivers beaten. Some accounts say that the name Purple Gang came from the gang's habit of throwing purple dye on the laundry of those failing to cooperate. Others claim it came from a news report in which a crime witness said the boys were "purple—like rotting meat."

Despite their brutal tactics, the thirteen Purple Gang members tried for extortion related to their involvement in the dry-cleaning war were acquitted. It was a big day for the newsies.

The gang's ruthless dealings during the Cleaners and Dyers War and the gang's 1927 Milaflores Massacre, the first machine gun killing in the city's underworld, developed the Purple Gang's merciless reputation, according to Kavieff. No one dared testify against them in court, making law enforcement helpless to prosecute them.

The gang's fierce tactics were known far and wide. Not even Chicago mobster Al "Scarface" Capone muscled onto their territory. Instead, the Midwest's biggest crime lords dealed. Capone claimed territory west of US 31 at Grand Rapids, from the Indiana border to Mackinac Straits, and the Purple Gang ran everything east of the line. With their smooth operation, the Detroit mobsters supplied Capone's liquor operations.

A report in the *Walkerville Times* explained a key component of the Purple Gang's business methods. "The gang developed the fictitious Art Novelty Company. Smuggled liquor coming into Detroit was repackaged and shipped under false label to St. Louis, Chicago, and other cities."

Purple Gang members are thought to have been "loaned" to Capone to carry out the infamous St. Valentine's Day Massacre in

Chicago in 1929, meant to send a message to Capone's rival gang. To say the Purple Gang was tough or brutal is an understatement. The group included men such as "Two Gun Harry," a gang enforcer and specialist with the knife and gun; "Harry the Hat," a ladies' man who seemed glued to his grey fedora and ran a series of night-clubs; and Joe "Legs" Laman, a specialist in kidnappings. Gunman Jack Stein came to Detroit from New York to join the gang, as did a roster of other enforcers and racketeers.

The gang operated a diverse crime network. Perhaps the most successful arm of the operation was the Gang's liquor operation. While the states prohibited alcohol consumption, Canadian law prohibited general use but allowed for its production and export. Detroit's waterfront thus became the hotbed for illegal liquor transport. Ever ready for an opportunity, the Purple Gang formed what became known as "The Jewish Navy" to hijack shipments of liquor crossing the waterways, shooting smugglers who failed to hand over the goods. Hijacking was such a frequent occurrence that fishermen and pleasure boaters were reluctant to go on the water for fear of getting caught in crossfire. In 1931, a passenger onboard the excursion ship the *Ste. Claire* was shot from stray bullets coming from a border patrol unit. Despite dangers to the public, the hijacking business took place year round. When the Detroit River froze, it formed a bootleg ice highway between Michigan and Ontario.

Both Detroit's underworld and its legitimate business community flourished during the Prohibition era. While Henry Ford, the iconic American industrialist and founder of the Ford Motor Company, demonstrated his ingenuity in Detroit's manufacturing world, bootleggers demonstrated their own kind of genius by smuggling liquor in imaginative ways. It came in beneath false floorboards in cars, second gas tanks, false-bottom suitcases and shopping baskets, and it was dragged beneath boats, wrote Jenny Nolan in the *Detroit News*. Liquor pipelines were built. "Between Peche Island and the foot of Alter Road, an electronically controlled cable hauled metal cylinders filled with up to 50 gallons of booze," Nolan reported. Another pipeline went from Windsor, Canada, directly to a Detroit bottler. Belle Isle was a key smuggling station along the river, and the warehouse district east of today's GM Renaissance Center was a hub for bootlegging business.

Prohibition laws clearly failed to quench Detroiters' taste for drink. In general, law enforcement took a lenient approach to illegal consumption and sales, and some became a part of the operations feeding the corruption problem. Liquor was easy for ordinary citizens to obtain. As many as twenty-five thousand speakeasies operated in Detroit in 1929. Some blocks had dozens of the joints, which residents called "blind pigs," and they ran the gamut from back-street operations to upscale clubs. The Stork Club on Rowena Street was considered one of the most exclusive blind pigs in Detroit and a favorite Purple Gang hang-out. According to Nolan, a blind pig above a bail bondsman's office across from Police Headquarters was frequented by police who had a penchant for the menu. When the Deutsches Haus at Mack and Maxwell was raided, arrests included Detroit Mayor John Smith, Michigan Congressman Robert Clancy, and Sheriff Edward Stein. Blue-collar autoworkers unwilling to give up their drink could buy a shot in the factory parking lot at Hamtramck.

The vice business was everywhere, and it was big business, indeed. The lucrative nature of bootlegging led to increased competition and violence between rival gangs as well as to infighting and treachery among Purple Gang members. An irreversible tide of viciousness and greed prevailed, culminating in what became known as the Collingwood Massacre.

The Collingwood incident involved gang members working for the "Jewish Navy"—Joseph Leibowitz, Herman "Hymie" Paul, and Isadore "Izzy the Rat" Sutker. The gang renegades wanted a bigger piece of the pie and began trespassing on other Purple Gang member territory and on rival mob business. Ray Bernstein arranged a meeting with the renegades, leading them to believe it was to be a peace meeting. Bookie Sol Levine escorted the rebels to the Collingwood boardinghouse on September 16, 1931. Instead of finding a platform for discussion, the three men were massacred. The gunmen safely escaped via an alley behind the building.

Crime ruled Detroit and also provided an element of dramatic entertainment for the everyday person. Following the shooting, scores of men, women, and children gathered around the Collingwood to witness the investigation.

Levine, the Collingwood shooter, later served as a state witness in the murder case against key gang members Ray Bernstein, Harry Keywell, and Irving Milberg. Each was convicted of first-degree murder and received life sentences.

Though the Collingwood Massacre was a high-profile incident, it was only one of many gang slayings during the period. Between 1927 and 1932, eighteen members of the Purple Gang were killed by other members of their own gang.

Police and spectators gather outside Boesky's delicatessen in Detroit after the 1937 fatal shooting of gangster Harry Millman.

Public tolerance for violence reached the tipping point in the early 1930s. The days of the Purple Gang's reign of the city were now on the decline. Once Prohibition was overturned in 1933, the black market for liquor collapsed and the gang's control over Detroit diminished. The 1937 shooting of gang member Harry Millman was considered the turning point leading to the demise of gangland's stronghold on the city. A gang enforcer with a reputation for being unpredictable, Millman had stepped on one too many toes. Both the Purple Gang and the Detroit Mafia wanted him out of the way. So it was no surprise when Millman was shot point blank on November 25, 1937, at a crowded restaurant.

With law enforcement cracking down and Purple Gang leaders imprisoned, other mob forces gained power in Detroit's labor racketeering, gambling, and drug trade. However, the Purple Gang didn't go down alone. According to Kavieff's account, Mayor Charles Bowles, a former Detroit Recorders judge with links to underworld dealings, was recalled. Then the leader of the recall movement, radio broadcaster Gerald Buckley, was assassinated by mobsters on July 23, 1930, in the lobby of the Detroit LaSalle Hotel as he sat reading a newspaper. Another government official rumored to be on the Purple Gang payroll was Henry J. Garvin, who served on the Detroit Police Department's crime and bomb squad. Garvin was the target of a murder attempt in January of the same year. Patrolman Vivian Welch, who was reportedly extorting money from the gang, also died at the hands of the gang.

With their Detroit influence disappearing, some of those who survived the underworld gangs moved on to greener pastures, taking murder and mayhem from the streets of Detroit to small-town Michigan. About 1938, organized crime found its way to central and northern Michigan spurred by an oil boom between Mt. Pleasant and Clare.

A key player in the mid-Michigan underworld operations was Isaiah Leebove. Leebove had built his reputation as an attorney for New York gangsters, according to a report in *The Oakland Press*. He was also a Purple Gang accomplice and involved with Jack Livingston, a wealthy oil prospector—a relationship that ultimately led to Leebove's demise. While sitting at a booth near the front window of the Tap Room at Clare's Doherty Hotel, Livingston pumped three bullets into Leebove.

Leebove's Clare home, complete with an underground escape tunnel to the Tobacco River, still stands and has become a public curiosity. *The Morning Sun* reported people have shown up at the property over the years hoping to uncover money Leebove supposedly hid at the site. In 2017, the public had an opportunity to view the property when it was featured in Clare's Art of Gardening Tour.

In Albion, long-time gang members Sam, Louis, and Harry Fleisher along with Sam Stone set up new crime operations. Even for aging gangsters, business was all about location, location, location. Halfway between Detroit and Chicago, the city of Albion had been a stopping point for Prohibition gangsters conducting operations with other Midwest mobsters. The Albion gang faction established Riverside Iron and Metal Company as a front operation for their safe-cracking business and other clandestine activities. The junkyard was strategically located along the Kalamazoo River. Today, the site is home to Thompson's Brakes and Suspension.

The gang also leased a stall at an auto storage building near the junkyard to keep their "super auto." It was a stolen Graham-Paige sedan they had cleverly converted into a crime mobile, with revolving license plates, bullet-proof glass, metal shields, and removable doors and seats to accommodate safes. It was reputedly used in a string of southern Michigan robberies.

Between crime sprees, the Albion gang met at the Bohm Theatre on Sunday evenings. The Streetcar Tavern was another favorite haunt. A converted inter-urban car, the tavern was adjacent to an apartment house owned by Louis and Abe "Buffalo Harry" Rosenberg.

Albion Downtown Development Authority remembers the mobsters by providing gang accounts to visitors and offering maps for walking tours of the gang's landmark sites, including the Riverside Iron and Metal Company site, the Bohm Theatre, the auto storage facility, and a former Kroger Grocery the gang robbed in 1936. Visitors can also trace the gang's steps along an alley off Clinton Street where the gangsters roughed-up enemies and made quick escapes. The Albion Police Station on Cass Street is highlighted as the spot the Albion gang was jailed after arrest for safe-cracking.

The Purple Gang reign came to a final end in 1945, with the assassination of Albion resident State Senator Warren G. Hooper. Hooper admitted he was one of several state legislators taking bribes from Republican party boss Frank McKay, who reportedly had strong connections to the Detroit underworld. At issue at the time was pending racetrack legislation with the potential to boost mob profits. Hooper was to testify against McKay in exchange for immunity. It is believed McKay put out a $25,000 contract on Hooper's life. On January 16, 1945, the senator was shot and killed in his car while driving home to Albion from Lansing. His death prevented his testimony of the alleged corruption in state legislature. Harry Fleisher, Sam Fleisher, and Myron "Mikey" Selik as well as several other associates were later convicted of conspiracy to murder Hooper.

After the Purple Gang disbanded, at least one former member remained a visible reminder of Detroit's violent past. Sam Solomon, once the Jewish Navy boss and operator of one of the town's largest bookmaking operations, bought a concession stand in the old Detroit Post Office, where the blind former gangster sold cigars.

The Purple Gang had bled itself to death, and Abe Bernstein finally surrendered power to the Italian mob.

As for Detroit's young newsies who spread word of gang slayings and arrests, life became easier when, in 1938, the federal Fair Labor Standards Act regulated minimum age and hours of work for children.

CHAPTER 11

The Buried City of Singapore

With ice skates jauntily slung over their shoulders, two boys wandered along the Lake Michigan beach making their way from Saugatuck to Macatawa. At Macatawa, they laced on their skates and glided along the frozen Black River to Holland. At mid-afternoon, the boys headed back home to Saugatuck, unwittingly closing a chapter of Michigan history.

The lake winds blew hard, fast, and cold on that day in the winter of 1894, chilling the boys to the bone. Along the route, they decided to build a bonfire to warm themselves, making a fire with the rooftop remnants of a long-deserted house. It wasn't just any house or stray debris the boys lit ablaze; it was the last visible remains of the buried city of Singapore.

Sometimes called "Michigan's Pompeii," the city beneath the sand, Singapore, was once a bustling little town with big dreams. But Singapore's vision of prosperity rose and fell within the period of a few decades, buried by changing times and its leaders' lack of foresight and greed, and then, finally, it was reclaimed by shifting sands.

Singapore's story begins with the opening of the Erie Canal in 1825, which launched the Territory of Michigan into an active period of development. The canal linked the Atlantic Ocean to the Great Lakes, opening the region to a promising new era in trade and settlement. Land speculators, the scrupulous and unscrupulous alike, competed for property and a role in this New World money game.

A confluence of factors led to Singapore's creation, including Michigan's quest for entry into the union and the new state's Wildcat Banking Law of 1837. The banking law permitted twelve or more landholders of any county to organize a bank with the minimum capital of $50,000. These "wildcat banks" had the right to print and issue money, and they were subject to only ambiguous regulations regarding the redemption of money. They earned the nickname wildcat banks because they were as "elusive as wildcats in the woods." According to legend, the location of one wildcat bank was a hollow tree stump. In all, forty Michigan banks established operations under the law.

One year before the law was enacted, forty-two-year-old Oshea Wilder, a resident of Eckford Township, Calhoun County, found four partners willing to invest $25,000 each in land purchases within the Great Lakes basin. Wilder hailed from Gardner, Massachusetts, and had served in the military during the War of 1812. He settled in Rochester, New York, before setting his hopes for prosperity on Michigan resources. A professional surveyor and blacksmith, the pioneer moved his wife and family of six to Michigan in 1832. By 1834, the ambitious entrepreneur was appointed by the territorial governor to a three-man commission tasked with the job of locating a county seat for Allegan County.

With investment funds, Wilder bought several parcels in Calhoun, Jackson, Hillsdale, and Allegan Counties, but the prize he desired most was property located at the mouth of the Kalamazoo River. In her book, *Buried Singapore: Michigan's Imaginary Pompeii,* Kit Lane quotes a letter Wilder wrote to one of his investors. "There is but two or three points of Lake Michigan of more importance than this for a town—Chicago and Milwalky on the west side are more valuable. Michigan City, St. Joseph and Grand River will be of very little more importance than this, and except Grand River, it has the best natural harbor on the east side of the Lake, and better than any on the other side—except Milwalky, of this I have no knowledge."

The land Wilder eyed was already owned by a New York native, H. H. Comstock, who also saw great promise in the location. Unable to work out a deal with Comstock, Wilder purchased half interest in 115 acres just to the north at the river's crook. Wilder and his investors decided the town they were about to plant would be called Singapore. Lane points out that no records exist as to why the men chose the unusual name for their settlement. Some say it was for the area's "singing sands," the unique feature found only along Lake Michigan's eastern shores, where the sand reverberates when stepped upon, creating a singing sound. Others claim it was named after the Asian city, an emerging center of trade.

In short order, Wilder had the town surveyed. It was plotted with streets named Cedar, Cherry, Detroit, and Broad north of the river, with streets named River, Oak, Pine, Chestnut, Walnut, and Beach intersecting them. Wilder planned construction of a sawmill, workers' quarters, and boats, and had secured contracts to deliver timber products to clients. Singapore's birth coincided with the Michigan Legislature's commitment to build the Clinton-Kalamazoo Canal across the state from Lake St. Clair on the east to near the new town. Singapore, it seemed, was poised to become a major Great Lakes port. It all looked very bright, indeed, until the Financial Panic of 1837 struck and the canal project was abandoned.

Without a crystal ball to see future pitfalls, Wilder viewed the passage of the Wildcat Banking Act as a stellar opportunity to grow the profitability of his city. Unable to interest his original New York backers in creating the Bank of Singapore, he enlisted local investors and family members in his effort. Wilder's son was named bank president, and the bank was located in a boarding-house. A New York engraver printed its money in $1, $2, $3, and $5 denominations. Singapore Bank opened books for subscription November 7 to 10, 1837. Residents viewed the new bank's ornate bills, printed only on one side, with considerable skepticism. *Lost & Found Ghost Towns of the Saugatuck Area,* co-authored by Kit Lane and Robert Simonds, quotes a resident: "The money was good enough at home, but you couldn't travel any farther than you could on a piece of bark."

Thousands of dollars of Singapore money was printed, but the bank was poorly backed. When inspectors appeared, bank operators were forced into a game of deceit. Locals relish the tale of the time Wilder colluded with a neighboring bank to falsely fill his coffer. As the inspector exited the Bank of Allegan, its gold was sent out the back door in a rush to reach Singapore before the examiner reached the city. Larry Massie highlighted the incident in his book *Copper Trails & Iron Rails*. "When Wilder got wind of the approach of a bank examiner, legend has it he temporarily borrowed specie from an Allegan bank. As the story goes, the canoe carrying the gold hit a snag in the Kalamazoo and the money bags sank to the bottom of the river." While en route to Singapore, the bank examiner was delayed with entertainment at a tavern while a blacksmith hurriedly forged a grapple hook to retrieve the gold to save the day.

In 1838, Michigan suspended banking laws allowing wildcat banks, putting these shaky organizations out of business. The Bank of Singapore charter and others were annulled in 1842. As a result, Singapore's currency literally went up in smoke. *Lost & Found: Ghost Towns of the Saugatuck Area* recounts the tale of Levi Loomis who claimed to be present when the town's bills were destroyed by tossing them into a burning stove. He commented in a local newspaper, "(They) sufficed for boiling a tea kettle twice."

Despite the troubled financial environment, Singapore was sustained by a handful of hardy settlers, in part by accident, or as some must have believed, a miracle. The winter of 1842 was unusually harsh along the lakeshore. Snows made roads impassable and food was in short supply. The wooden steamer *Milwauki* became beached in a violent storm just two miles north of Singapore, claiming the lives of several sailors. Fortunately for the folks of Singapore, the ship's cargo of flour was salvaged, some of it stored locally and shared by its owners, saving residents from starvation.

When the nation's rocky economy began to rebound in 1844, Singapore's sawmill, earlier consumed by fire, was rebuilt. The region's valuable pine harvest fueled town expansion as it helped build and rebuild Midwestern cities. The community by now consisted of about a dozen dwellings, Lane reported in her book. Singapore was ready to boom. Mill owners Francis Browne Stockbridge and Artemis Carter decided they needed a vessel to transport lumber to market. To accomplish the goal, they contracted the construction of the *Octavia,* a handsome three-masted schooner.

During this period, Singapore was home to between one hundred and two hundred people. It was clearly a company town with most of the population consisting of millworkers and their families. Twenty-two buildings lined its streets, including three mills, two hotels, and general stores. Like other towns of the era, the wooden structures were highly vulnerable to fire, and on May 20, 1866, tragedy struck Singapore. Fire consumed five houses and a sawmill. Three years later, the largest mill of all was built to replace it.

Demand for lumber remained strong, and Singapore grew. Its shining moment came in the period following the Civil War. Massie wrote: "In 1870 alone, 672 vessels cleared the mouth of the Kalamazoo carrying 30 million feet of lumber, 31 million shingles and other wood products."

Ships carrying lumber from Singapore to Chicago returned without cargo. Mill owner Francis Stockbridge and his partner Otis Johnson realized they could increase profits by bringing in raw hides from Chicago stockyards to create a two-way payload. They contracted construction of the three-masted schooner, the *O. R. Johnson.* She set sail in 1868, making the Chicago run in seven to ten hours. Lane reported that in the ship's first season, she made 57 trips in 232 days and carried 6.7 million board feet of lumber. Two

In 1869, Singapore's sawmill operations feed construction in Midwest towns.

COURTESY OF SAUGATUCK-DOUGLAS HISTORICAL SOCIETY

more schooners and two barges were later added to the Singapore fleet.

Singapore's mills and fleet hummed along, feeding the need for lumber to rebuild nearby Holland and Chicago, both of which were devastated by fire in 1871. The intense demand heralded Singapore's unforeseen end. Once the region's woods were stripped bare and its natural wealth consumed, the sawmills closed. Mill equipment was loaded onto a handful of vessels to reestablish operations at St. Ignace.

Just one month after the mills were shuttered, the town was on life support. The once thriving community was barely breathing, fast disappearing, board by board. Folks hauled the homes and businesses away either in whole or piece by piece. Entire buildings were pulled by horses across the frozen river to Saugatuck. The structures that once lined Broad, Cherry, Chestnut, and other friendly streets were now addresses at a different town. The old wildcat bank building was relocated to north Saugatuck and transformed into a general store. It was moved again around 1890 to downtown Saugatuck, where it served various purposes over time, including a boardinghouse, store, art gallery, and book shop. By 1890, little more than fifty years after Wilder had dreamed up the town, all that stood of consequence was the boardinghouse. It was too large to relocate. James Nichols, a fisherman, moved into the deserted three-story structure and kept watch over the town until the bitter end.

Without its original tree covering, coastal sands blew freely, gradually covering Singapore's remains.

As in Singapore's era, the natural effects of wind and waves continue to affect Michigan's 275,000 acres of dune formations. When void of protective vegetation, winds blow shoreward at speeds of eight to twenty-five miles per hour, moving sand grains along the dune system. Storms and lake levels cause rapid natural changes along these vulnerable dunes. So sensitive are the dunes that in 1989 the state enacted the Sand Dunes Protection and Management Program for their protection. The legislation regulates commercial, residential, and industrial development with potential to alter dune ecology. But in the mid-1800s, dune conservation was a concept still more than a century away.

Left ravaged by logging and compromised by development, Singapore silently succumbed to the natural movement of shifting sands. When the first floor of the Singapore hotel filled with sand,

Nichols moved up to the next, and when that floor was swallowed by sand, he located to the third floor. Finally, the fisherman, like all the others, was forced to abandon his home. He was the last man out of a city destined for demise from its beginning.

Mother Nature recaptured the land, leaving few traces of the town to be found. But for a while, clues to its past surfaced. High water during the 1970s exposed the floor of the west sawmill as well as dock supports. Bits of glass and pottery, the remains of lives long faded away, were also found. Through 1980, the careful observer could detect sand mounds where buildings had once stood. Eventually, Mother Nature prevailed and the town of Singapore became simply a footprint in Michigan history.

Some compare Singapore to the Italian city of Pompeii, buried by the eruption of Mt. Vesuvius. Located near the Bay of Naples, Pompeii was graced with natural resources, namely soil so rich its yield far exceeded that of any other locale in the region. Its economy and culture flourished with trade, and it served as a playground to the rich. On August 24, in the year AD 79, that all came to an abrupt end. Vesuvius exploded with a fury of ash, rock, and mud. Its steaming mess and suffocating fumes rained down on the town, burying the once prosperous community under thirty feet of volcanic deposits. To anyone paying attention, the volcano had provided warning. Four days before the end, Vesuvius rumbled a forewarning of disaster. Those not heeding the signal were buried alive in a matter of hours.

Those paying attention may also have foreseen the end to Singapore. Ray Nies, one of the boys responsible for the bonfire that had sent the remains of Singapore's hotel up in smoke, told his story during Saugatuck's centennial celebration. Lane quotes the letter Nies wrote to the community, which was published in the local press: "Little did the builders of Singapore dream that the end of their imposing edifice would be to warm up a couple of tramps. But many large projects come to ignominious ends."

These wise words could be repeated many times up and down Michigan's coastline. Native Americans for several thousand years lived here in harmony with the natural world. The land and rivers provided all they needed to survive. But after the Erie Canal opened, Europeans settling Michigan brought a different philosophy. The state's forest wealth was viewed as a commodity to serve their own purposes. Like Singapore, logging villages popped up along the shoreline with docks, steamships, boardinghouses, general stores, and blacksmith shops to facilitate lumber trade. The towns included places like Aral, Edgewater, Good Harbor, and North Unity. As many as five hundred people might have populated a village, and if the residents were ambitious, the towns would have a school, a post office, and a church.

By 1910, the trees were gone—cut down, sawed, and shipped far from the forests. The logging boom ended. Active villages were abandoned. As it turned out, the short-term vision of Singapore's founders and the logging industry created only limited wealth and short-term jobs. Without a plan to manage the resources in a sustainable manner, prosperity disappeared.

Singapore vanished so completely, it prompts historic commemoration. Its bitter memory and that of other Michigan ghost towns begs us to raise our awareness of the consequences we face in squandering our natural resources without consideration for future generations.

CHAPTER 12

Legends of the Forest

The mid-1930s was a pivotal time in Michigan history. Organized labor came of age. The International Blue Water Bridge opened, connecting Port Huron to Sarnia, Ontario, Canada. To top it off, the Detroit Tigers won the World Series. But while the state had plenty to celebrate, ordinary folks were recovering from hard times stemming from the Great Depression.

Robert Fortney was one of those folks. The summer of 1938 found the seventeen-year-old Cadillac resident without a job and with time on his hands. An unexplained encounter he had as he whiled away the hours of a midsummer day was so startling that he kept the incident secret for almost fifty years.

Fortney was fishing along the Muskegon River near Paris in Mecosta County. The second largest river in the state, the Muskegon is a rich fishery winding through the Manistee National Forest in the western edge of the county. Fortney's peace and quiet was suddenly interrupted by a pack of feral dogs making their way out of the woods lining the river banks. The teenager froze, hoping the dogs would not notice him. Maybe the wind was not in his favor and carried his scent to the pack. It just wasn't his lucky day, for the wild pack moved in closer to him.

Fortney picked up his loaded hunting rifle and fired a shot into the air to scare the dogs off. It worked. The pack stole back into the forest—all except one. A huge, black dog with piercing eyes stood not ten feet from the angler. Fortney fired a second shot into the air. The beast didn't flinch. Instead, the dog reared up on its hind legs and cast a look Fortney never forgot. "I swear the dog was smiling at me," he told interviewers, according to www.absolute michigan.com. The monster dog backed down, then rejoined his pack. Shaken to the core, the young man waited decades to speak of the incident.

Fortney's tale is one of the early recorded accounts of human encounters with the Michigan Dogman, but not the earliest. Hints of the Dogman legend emerge in Native American tales. In 1784, French fur traders working in the region recounted stories of *loup garou,* a human with the ability to change into a wolf at will. Later, a Dogman creature gave men from a logging camp in Wexford County the scare of their lives. Eleven lumberjacks working near Garland Swamp came upon an animal they believed was a common dog. According to the legend recounted at www.northernexpress .com, the men chased the animal into a hollow log. One lumberjack poked at the beast inside the log until it released an ungodly scream and emerged on two legs. The terrified men vacated camp immediately.

Reports of Dogman sightings have surfaced throughout the past one hundred years. In 1967, two fishermen were casting lines from a rowboat on Claybank Lake in Manistee County. They were about to head back to shore when one of the anglers noticed an animal swimming in their direction. As it approached the boat, the men were horrified to see the animal paddling with all fours had a humanlike face. As the creature came within a few feet of the boat, it grabbed the side and tried to climb aboard. One of the men began beating the creature's paws to loosen its grip. Finally, the beast gave up and let go. The frightened fisherman sped to shore. When later questioned by news reporters, they said little.

Other incidents occurring across the Mitten's north came to light, including one at Fife Lake in 1969, St. Helen in 1979, Reed City in 1993 and 2006, Antrim County in 2009, and Dowagiac in 2009.

Dogman legends retreated somewhat from popular culture until April Fool's Day 1987 rolled around. Traverse City WTCM radio personality Jack O'Malley wanted to dream up a joke to play on listeners. To help the cause, O'Malley's production director Steve Cook wrote a song embodying Dogman sightings. Just for fun, he threw in a warning to watch for Dogman to appear every seventh year of every decade. Cook recorded his song, "The Legend," and it hit the airwaves April first. Not only did the song eventually sell thousands of copies, but Cook also started receiving personal accounts of Dogman encounters, more than one hundred, in fact.

"The Legend" immortalized a 1987 sighting near the small town of Luther in Lake County. In that case, local law enforcement officers responded to a report of an animal attack at a cabin located just outside of town. Officers found the cabin's doors and windows torn apart, gnawed, shredded, scratched, and punctured. Most unexplainable, teeth marks were visible on the building at a height of seven feet. The only clue to the perpetrator was tracks of a large dog found at the site. The Luther attack made national news and was the focus of a Paul Harvey nationwide broadcast. The north woods became a formidable place to more than a few Michiganders.

In 1989, Cook created a sequel to his song, titled "The Sigma Story." The sequel tells of a town in Kalkaska County that vanishes after a pack of Dogmen appear.

Twenty years and one day after first airing the original Dogman song, the final version of "The Legend" debuted on WTCM. What began as a joke now fueled the legend for a new generation. Since first hitting the airwaves, Cook has donated thousands of dollars of song profits to area charities, primarily animal rescue groups and other service organizations.

Cook's "The Legend" seems to have a life of its own. It has spawned screenplays, stage productions, and books. In 2009, the History Channel filmed an hour-long program called *American Werewolf* for its MonsterQuest series. Filmed on location in northern Michigan, the documentary featured eyewitness accounts and linked Dogman to a similar beast in Wisconsin. The crew spent several days near Luther creating a reenactment, according to the *Traverse City Record Eagle.*

Although intended to uncover the truth behind the Dogman legend, the film failed to put the mystery to rest. Some Dogman believers claim the creature is linked to the Native American tradition of shapeshifting, the human ability to transform into an animal shape, often a wolf, coyote, or owl. When in animal form, the shapeshifter takes on the attributes of the animal. In Native American culture, the phenomenon is associated with hunting, war, healing, song, and dance.

Some curious souls wonder whether shapeshifters could also be behind Bigfoot sightings in the Manistee Forest and beyond. While a high percentage of Dogman reports come from the national forest and surrounding counties within the northwest section of the Lower Peninsula, Bigfoot sightings are more widespread. However, in July 2009, Ron Kostrubiec experienced what he believed was a Bigfoot encounter at Wilderness State Park in Emmet County along Little Traverse Bay, about thirty miles south of Mackinac Straits.

Kostrubiec was biking through the northern landscape along Swamp Lake Trail in the early evening hours. The *Petoskey News* reported that two miles into his trek, Kostrubiec ran into a wall of "foul odor." He told the news reporter, "It sent chills up my spine and my hair stood up. It scared me so much, I peddled out of there as fast as I could."

Kostrubiec returned to the site the next evening to investigate and found the odor had disappeared. "That tells me something was there. And I truly believe whatever was there watched me go by," Kostrubiec said.

He returned to the site each night of the family's stay but was unable to find other clues to the mystery. Word of the sighting got around the campground, and it came to light that a young camper had experienced a foul body odor near the campground the same day Kostrubiec had stumbled into it. Kostrubiec was

An artist's image of the Michigan Dogman

destined to get one more clue. Just before the vacation ended, while on a hike the family came upon unusual markings on the forest floor. They followed the markings to the base of a fallen tree, where they spotted a clear footprint sixteen inches long and very wide with each toe clearly visible. A hunter and fisherman who had spent a great deal of time in the woods of both the Lower and Upper Peninsulas, Kostrubiec had never encountered anything like it before.

Kostrubiec isn't alone in his experience. The Bigfoot Field Researchers Organization (BFRO) has recorded a total of 122 plausible sightings coming from 54 of Michigan's 83 counties. Counties with the highest number of reports are Marquette (7), Ogemaw (6), Oscoda (8), Schoolcraft (8), and Washtenaw (6).

BFRO is dedicated to solving the Bigfoot mystery through field and laboratory investigations. The organization maintains that North American Bigfoot sightings have been reported for four hundred years, many from highly credible sources. Native American tribes passed down legends of the hairy creature quite similar to descriptions of the beast related by modern eyewitnesses. Only in the past seventy years has it been possible to provide substantial photographic evidence and footprint castings of the legendary creature's remarkably large, human-shaped tracks.

Bigfoot skeptics argue that reports of giant tracks and sightings of unusual creatures are due to misidentification of common animal species. BFRO members see it another way. They believe reports suggest the presence of an unidentified primate species. Believers in the seven-hundred–pound mystery man of the forest include anthropologists, biologists, and wildlife experts.

Eyewitness composites suggest Bigfoot is a seven- or eight-foot, hairy, apelike creature with an offensive odor. Numerous witnesses have reported hearing the creature make loud guttural sounds in a low tone. Unlike a bear, it maintains an upright position, walking with a long stride and a lumbering gait.

BFRO member Phil Shaw of West Branch is a Bigfoot hunter. According to *The Ogemaw County Herald,* his interest in the mythical creature was inspired by a sighting he experienced during a 2006 vacation in another state. He now joins BFRO expeditions in search of the elusive being.

"It takes a lot to connect with these animals. If you've got a pretty remote area, they're likely to be less intimidated or reclusive. If there's not a lot of people, they could be curious," Shaw told the *Herald.*

Shaw points out that Bigfoot's need for good water sources make Michigan swamplands an ideal habitat for the shy creatures. He surmises they have good night vision and are likely herbivores.

BFRO theorizes Bigfoot lives in a small and mobile family group. Leaving little impact on the land, they are difficult for untrained individuals to catch sight of. The low profile results in relatively few human encounters. When they are spotted, it is often in a forested area with a large deer population.

Bigfoot, known in some circles as Sasquatch, Yeti, or the Abominable Snowman, is more than a good campfire story, according to many experts, including world-famous chimpanzee researcher Jane Goodall. Goodall made her view known when she told an interviewer from National Public Radio that she believed undiscovered primates such as Yeti or Sasquatch exist.

You don't have to convince Cindy Barone of rural St. Clair County. Her Bigfoot story went nationwide in 1981, via news wire services. A November 22 article published in *The Detroit News* describes a frightening encounter at the Barone farm. One fall evening Barone's teenage daughter, Tina, and her younger daughter, Roxanne, went to the barn to check on the animals. Tina moved to turn on the lights, but instead of feeling the familiar switch beneath her fingers, she felt fur. When the lights came on, she found herself standing next to a tall, hairy animal. She told reporters the creature stood two feet above her and glared down at her with "bright red eyes." The Bigfoot apparently liked farm living. The Barone farm fences were repeatedly torn down, and the animals spooked on several occasions.

Despite thousands of reported Bigfoot sightings in North America over a period of several centuries, conclusive evidence pointing to its existence is lacking. In 2003, *National Geographic* news reported that some members of the scientific community insist Bigfoot calls for serious study. "They propose that there's enough forensic evidence to warrant something that has never been done: a comprehensive scientific study to determine if the legendary primate actually exists."

In his paper "Sasquatch & Scientists: Reporting Scientific Anomalies," Eastern Michigan University's Dr. Ron Westrum, a Harvard-trained sociologist, pointed out the significance of scientific validation in the Bigfoot matter. "It is science that decides what is real and what is not, what exists and what does not exist. To be sure, other institutions compete with science for this right, but ultimately, science is the arbiter. When the reality of creatures like Sasquatch is put to the question, science has the final say. Even Sasquatch advocates who have nothing good to say about science would be delighted if science would admit these hypothetical creatures to the realm of legitimately researchable objects."

Westrum points out the dilemma a Bigfoot eyewitness faces following an unverified experience. They often question their own perceptions and must decide whether to share their observations and face possible ridicule as well as with whom to share the information, or to just keep quiet. If they make a public statement, they also run the risk of it being attacked as a hoax.

To be fair, Bigfoot has been the brunt of frequent pranksters and hoaxes. In 2008, Kalamazoo native Philip Morris confessed to his role in perpetuating a hoax lasting more than forty years. A costume maker for movie studios, he one day received a call requesting a Neanderthal gorilla suit, Morris told the *Kalamazoo Gazette*. "He said the costume was for a prank, but I thought that it was pretty odd because these were expensive suits." Nonetheless, Morris sent the suit and even offered advice to the customer on how to create the illusion of looking larger by using pads and brushing up the fur.

Two months later, Morris saw the customer interviewed on television along with footage of someone wearing the costume. The customer claimed the footage was that of Bigfoot and that he'd filmed it while hunting in northern California. Morris chose to maintain his client's confidentiality, waiting until the man died before going public. The *Gazette* quoted Morris saying, "Most people believe me, but there are people very hostile to me when I tell them it is a hoax. It is like telling them Santa Claus doesn't exist. They grew up believing it was true and do not want to admit to themselves it's fake."

In the Upper Peninsula Bark River area located in Menominee County, the Native American population has little doubt they share the woods with "Harry," as he is known in those parts. Many have had personal encounters, but few choose to share these experiences with outsiders. In the fall of 2009, one Native American couple decided to make a statement and reported multiple sightings to MFRO. The case was investigated and documented by MFRO's Don Peer.

According to Peer's report, when the sighting occurred the older couple wasn't hunting, hiking, or seeking a Bigfoot experience. They were simply enjoying a quiet evening at home watching deer graze in the open space outside of their large bay window. Around 7:00 p.m., they noticed a spooked deer run off. Their first thoughts were that a wolf, coyote, or hunter had wandered onto the property. They grabbed binoculars to get a closer look. What they saw was a dark figure, six or seven feet tall, wander into view. The couple knew immediately it wasn't human, even though it walked upright, occasionally stooping, as if looking for food. After a half-hour's time, the strange figure disappeared into the surrounding forest.

Only a few nights earlier, one of the witnesses had smelled "a skunky musty smell in the air," according to the case file, and had experienced a sense of unease when he went out to the backyard. Over the period of two years, the same witnesses spotted "Harry" on three occasions.

The investigator learned that Native Americans in the area have great respect for their Bigfoot neighbors and seek only to live in harmony with the creatures. Whether Bigfoot and Dogman are true unidentified species or figments of our collective imagination, that seems like a good attitude to adopt.

CHAPTER 13

The Truth behind Michigan's Muses

Eight muses dressed in flowing robes peer down from the Michigan State Capitol's inner dome, reflecting state economic and social ideals. But the painter of these iconic figures never stepped foot in Michigan. In fact, the artist's identity was hidden from the public for more than a century.

Michigan's muses were installed in the Capitol dome in 1886, the same year the Statue of Liberty was dedicated in New York Harbor. The dome's ladies in white were the crowning glory of Lansing's Neoclassical capitol building constructed between 1872 and 1878. The elegant building was designed to replicate elements of the nation's capitol in Washington, DC, and served as a model for numerous statehouses. In 1992, the Michigan Capitol's architectural and artistic significance earned it the National Park Service designation of National Historic Landmark.

Construction of the ornate capitol building came at a time when the young state desired to develop its standing as a sophisticated and worldly player. At its completion, the building featured nine acres of hand-painted columns, doors, wainscots, cornices, and ceilings, which are considered some of the finest examples of Victorian decorative painting. But the new statehouse carried a high price tag. The modest construction budget of $1.5 million left nothing for adorning the interior. Eventually, clever measures were employed when decorating funds were later appropriated. To create a lavish ambiance, the interior's cheap pine, plaster, and cast iron were painted to resemble the richness of marble and walnut. Gilding, stenciling, glazing, and marbling transformed the capitol's plain spaces into an architectural jewel.

Meanwhile, the muses harbored a secret of their own. The story of their true origin only slowly unraveled after the state launched a capitol renovation project in 1987. The multiyear major restoration included rehabilitation of the muse paintings.

When it came to the creation of the muses, state records were incomplete. Documents fail to list the building's project subcontractors, so clues to the muses' history were few and far between. It took a persistent team of art wizzes to crack the mystery of who painted Michigan's inspirational ladies and to discover exactly what each symbolized.

Like the thousands who visit the celebrated capitol every year, Taylor, Michigan, resident Reverend Geoffrey G. Drutchas made a pilgrimage to the state government seat in 1992. At that time, the muses were mistakenly attributed to another artist. But Drutchas had a hunch about their true origin and was driven to uncover the painter's identity, which lay buried deep in political history.

Drutchas had stumbled upon an announcement in a 1905 arts magazine that stated an Italian artist named Tommaso Juglaris received a commission at the Michigan Capitol. Spurred on by curiosity, Drutchas initiated a conversation about Juglaris with the Capitol Director of Tours and Capitol Historian Kerry Chartkoff. The exchange kicked off a serious quest to pinpoint who really created the capitol's extraordinary ladies who look over the building's art, architecture, and visitors.

The capitol's National Historic Landmark application acknowledges the statehouse's distinctive art: "So skillful and elaborate were the techniques and patterns employed, and so effective their color palette, that the building, as now restored, ranks today as one of the best surviving displays in the United States of the Victorian painted decorative arts."

In full detective mode, Chartkoff and Drutchas followed history's breadcrumbs until their quest led to a big reveal: the uncovering of the actual creator of Michigan's allegorical muses.

History's first breadcrumb links to the capitol's architect. In 1872, the Michigan Building Board of Commissioners approved funds for the new statehouse. Elijah E. Myers, an unknown architect at the time, competed for the opportunity to design the capitol building, Michigan's third government house. The first was constructed at Detroit, Michigan's capital city until Lansing received the designation in 1847. In late 1847, a temporary capitol building was hastily constructed in Lansing, which Michigan outgrew.

Myers's design for the new statehouse was one of twenty submitted. Once he won the design contract, the Springfield, Illinois, architect moved to Michigan, where he rolled up his sleeves and went to work on his architectural masterpiece. The project's subsequent success served to launch his career as the country's most prolific designer of public buildings. At the end of his career, his design portfolio included numerous statehouses and a hundred courthouses. It's thanks to Myers that domed state capitol buildings became the signature of US democracy.

It was the post–Civil War period when Myers received the capitol building commission. The architect desired to establish a statehouse that honored Michigan's effort in preserving the Union. Historians believe it was to that end that he modeled the Michigan Capitol after the United States Capitol in Washington, DC. As in the US Capitol, Myers incorporated an iron dome as the structure's centerpiece.

The National Historic Landmark document describes the Michigan Capitol dome: "The ribbed dome is punctuated by windows and topped by an elegant octagonal lantern, in turn topped by a two-layered set of bracketed cornices and a final ball and finial." It goes on to state, "The overall effect is simple and restrained, without unnecessary ornamentation as the original building commissioners demanded, but fine attention to detail and skillful execution has produced results which are both rich and subtle."

Materials for the new capitol structure were sourced from across the country. Stone came from Ohio, cast iron from Pennsylvania. Vermont provided marble and limestone for floors. On January 1, 1879, the building was dedicated to Michigan residents. According to the official capitol guidebook, speaking at its dedication, Governor Croswell said that the building stood as "evidence of the lasting taste, spirit and enterprise" of the citizens of the state.

The Gilded Age design exceeded the conservative budget. Nothing remained in the coffers to fund the interior ornamental touches that later drew so much praise and created a legacy. When the new capitol was dedicated, its walls were blank and bleak. It was six more years before the state coughed up the money to decorate the building.

The Capitol Decoration Commission, consisting of the governor, the auditor general, and the board of state auditors, put their heads together and at last approved an expenditure of $25,000 to embellish the Senate and House chambers, rotunda, Supreme Court chamber, governor's reception room, and first-floor front entrance corridor. Decorative artists from across the country competed for the prestigious job. In 1885, William Wright's Detroit firm was hired to add the finishing touches to Michigan's pride and joy.

Wright was another breadcrumb for the art detectives, but it didn't lead directly to the muse painter's identity. Wright pursued the nation's leading artists skilled in Victorian decorative techniques for work on the Michigan Capitol building, although it remains unclear how he selected the muse artist. During his entire lifetime, he kept the artist's identity under wraps. Without government access to Wright's old business records, which would likely have cited subcontractors including the muse artist, the public was forced to wait more than a hundred years for the secret to come to light.

Capitol historians believe Wright followed Myers's architectural design, which called for decorative art imitating the wall and ceiling art of the US Capitol. Painted figures in the US Capitol were created by Italian artist Constantino Brumidi. Brumidi contributed his talent to the US Capitol from the 1860s into the

1870s. According to the US Architect of the Capitol, Brumidi found his inspiration in the wall paintings of ancient Rome and Pompeii, as well as works from the Renaissance and Baroque periods. He integrated the classical and allegorical in portraits, giving a nod to the nation's values and inventions. Brumidi's Washington, DC, capitol paintings pay tribute to geography, history, liberty, peace, physics, and the telegraph.

Like Brumidi's figures, Michigan's muses reflect a fusion of the classical and allegorical. Dressed in flowing ancient Greek-style robes and seated on low walls or thrones, each Michigan muse holds an item pertaining to a theme and each is surrounded by related symbolic objects. Just as the artist's identity was a mystery, the muse themes remained a puzzle until the art sleuths researched seventeenth-century iconography text. The text documented symbols used by artists since before the European Renaissance and which appear in the Michigan muse paintings.

Until Drutchas discovered the lynchpin clue, Michigan artist Lewis Ives was believed to be the muse artist. Ives designed the rotunda pediment, which led to the widely held belief that he also painted the ladies of the inner dome. Ives's work was among the Detroit Institute of Arts (DIA) collection, and because the DIA restoration team on the capitol project was familiar with Ives's art, they were able to denounce him as the muse creator.

Chartkoff suspected the muse artist had long been misidentified, but he had no proof. The determined gumshoe Drutchas traveled to Italy in 2000, where he investigated the theory that connected Tommaso Juglaris to the capitol art once and for all. In a private collection of known Juglaris works, Drutchas found

The Muse of Arts is one of eight allegorical figures decorating the Michigan
Capitol building's inner dome. The muses held a secret for more than a century.

the breadcrumb that finally exposed the truth. He observed that the Italian artist's works contain a symbol likened to a stick figure. This mark also appeared on four muse sketches later found among the artist's papers in Italy. Upon further research, the art detectives learned that what was initially interpreted as a stick figure was a stylized version of Juglaris's initials. Finally, Juglaris was credited for his contribution to Michigan's art legacy.

The mystery of who painted Michigan's muses was at last solved. Case closed? Only partly. Another compelling piece of the mystery remained. Why was the identity of this acclaimed artist hidden from the Michigan public?

The capitol building's long-held secret when uncovered revealed Juglaris as a victim of the times in which he lived and worked. While Michigan was developing a modern reputation in the nation and world, the young artist destined for America was coming of age in Italy. Born in 1844 in the village of Moncalieri, Tommaso Juglaris grew up impoverished but managed to attend art school in Turin, Italy, between 1859 and 1862. Forced to quit due to lack of funds, he moved on to serve as apprentice to fresco artist Paolo Emilio Mongari. Juglaris developed his skills under Mongari by painting murals for churches, palaces, theaters, and civic buildings. In 1871, the artist moved to Paris, where he painted stage scenery before taking a job as a ceramics designer. The factory closed just a few years later, forcing Juglaris to redirect his career toward becoming an illustrator and industrial artist.

A major turning pointing in the artist's career came in 1880, when he received a job offer for work in the United States. Juglaris marked a new chapter in his life by accepting the position of art director for Louis Prang and Company, a Boston lithographer.

Despite the artist's high hopes for cultivating his career in the New World, the Prang job ended badly after six months. Juglaris chose to continue to pursue his career in America, working from his Boston studio. He exhibited and taught at prestigious art schools. He took up crafting stained glass for public buildings and churches, and became known as one of America's top decorative artists.

Juglaris fit the bill when Wright sought the nation's leading artists skilled in Victorian decorative techniques for work on the capitol's most visible and inspirational space: the inner dome.

Without ever visiting the Michigan Capitol, Juglaris began tackling the high-status job in April 1886 from his Boston studio. The eight muses bound for the dome were painted on canvas. The artist's use of live models resulted in dynamic portrayals of the allegorical figures installed as Michigan marked fifty years of statehood. Five months after he began the project, Juglaris shipped the first muse painting to Lansing, where it was hung to affirm the art appropriately enhanced the dome. By January, all of the eight muses were complete and secured to eight of the dome's niches.

However, the process was not without hurdles. The canvas paintings didn't quite cover the niches designated for them. To compensate, pieces of canvas were added and painted brown to form foundations for the figures. It's unclear whether a measuring mistake led to the problem or, as some surmise, looms of the period were unable to manufacture canvas in the needed size. Gold decorative panels were installed between the iconic ladies.

Whether it was Wright's decision or that of state authorities, the identity of the muse painter was clearly buried. This prestigious government job Juglaris thought would earn him recognition, fame, and lucrative American commissions did not deliver the anticipated rewards. Historians attribute it to the era's politics.

The muses took their place at the capitol during a national period of labor turmoil known as "The Great Upheaval." In May 1886, the same year Juglaris painted Michigan's muses, the Chicago "Haymarket Affair" marked one of the nation's most infamous years of labor conflict. The rally involved foreign-born activists fighting for eight-hour work days and better working conditions. The protest resulted in a clash between activists and Chicago police. Eight activists were arrested and convicted without solid evidence in a trial that drew months of national headlines. The trial resulted in seven of the activists receiving death sentences. The eighth was sentenced to fifteen years in prison. In the end, four of the men were hanged, and one died from suicide. The three activists still living had their sentences commuted.

The trial fed public fears regarding the patriotism and political motivation of foreign-born workers. An anti-immigrant and nativism environment that had been mounting since the 1840s became inflamed. Nationalists played on people's fear of diversity, and of the customs and beliefs of other cultures. Labor groups complained immigrants kept wages low.

It was in this political climate that in May 1887 State of Michigan legislators passed a law prohibiting non-citizen immigrants from working on publicly funded projects, like the state capitol building. Juglaris, who retained citizenship of his native Italy, was part of the banned labor force. Despite his stellar contribution to the capitol building, his immigrant status proved an embarrassment to the state government and likely prompted the hundred-year cover-up.

The artist's frustration with the Michigan project's failure to generate high status and lucrative commissions, compounded by the death of his wife and daughter, clouded his American life. In the following years, Juglaris commuted between Boston and Europe. In addition to the Michigan Capitol muses, his American legacy includes a commissioned portrait of First Lady Frances Folsom Cleveland, painted in 1890, and murals for the Ray Memorial Building / Franklin Library at Franklin, Massachusetts. Juglaris departed America for the last time in 1906 without ever having visited Michigan, the state where his paintings have inspired generations.

The uncovering of Juglaris as the Michigan muse painter spawned renewed interest in the artist on both sides of the Atlantic. New art pieces by Juglaris were discovered in both his native land and the United States. Because of revived appreciation for the artist's work, he finally received due credit. His pivotal role in connecting European and American artistic systems was acknowledged.

The artist's newly elevated status led to an international exhibition titled *Tommaso Juglaris: A Capitol Artist*. It featured fifty of the artist's paintings and sketches. The first international exhibit ever hosted by Lansing's Michigan Historical Museum was held from October 2004 to January 2005. It celebrated the restored muses and marked the Michigan Capitol's 125th anniversary. A coordinated exhibit was hosted by the Famija Moncalerisa cultural institute in the artist's hometown of Moncalieri, Italy, in 2006. The Italian-American organizations of metro Detroit commemorated the "Year of Italian Culture in the United States 2013" with an exhibition titled *Artist & Muses: Tommaso Juglaris and the Italian Legacy at Michigan's State Capitol*. It was co-curated by Drutchas and Chartkoff.

Visit the capitol building to view Michigan's muses liberated from their long-held secret. There's no charge for sixty-minute guided tours and self-guided tours of the capitol's public areas. Tours take place Monday through Saturday. They showcase the dome/rotunda, the gallery of the governors, the senate gallery, the governor's office, and the historic supreme court chamber.

The Muses and Their Themes

Michigan's muses continue to watch over capitol visitors. They embody the state's abiding vision, from its past to its present. Each of the contemplative figures holds an object related to her theme. Five muses are backdropped by blue skies or a starry night, while three sit silhouetted by a majestic throne or billowed sails. Their solemn aura and quiet colors provoke thoughtful consideration of Michigan's progress since they began presiding over the people of the Great Lakes State.

Agriculture: Seated beneath a blossoming tree and crowned with a wheat wreath, the Muse of Agriculture holds a shovel. At her feet are a bounty of fruits and vegetables.

Arts: Blue skies backdrop the Muse of Arts who holds an artist's palette, paintbrushes, and a plumb bob. Beside her is a statue of the goddess of wisdom and arts, Athena.

Astronomy/Science: The Muse of Science sits beneath a starry sky and holds a pen. Beside her are a telescope and world globe.

Commerce: The first muse installed, Commerce wears a winged headdress and holds a staff symbolizing safe passage. Beside her is a world globe and behind her are the opened sails of a ship.

Education: The Muse of Learning holds a ball symbolizing open-mindedness. She is surrounded by books, a compass, a scroll, a burning lamp, and a figure of a monkey or ape, which in early iconography language signifies arts and letters.

Industry: Industry's muse is backdropped by factories with smoking stacks. Beside her are a hammer, anvil, and machine parts.

Justice: Only the Muses of Astronomy/Science and Justice are portrayed with direct gazes. Justice is backdropped by a throne. Experts believe the artist modified this muse to broaden its theme into representing philosophy, which is signified by symbols on the tablet she holds.

The Muse of Law is also backdropped by a throne and night sky. She holds a scale of justice and a sword symbolizing the role of law in defending truth.

CHAPTER 14

Lighthouse Keepers from the Beyond

The romanticized picture of life as a Great Lakes lighthouse keeper is an overrated legend. In reality, the job was fraught with challenge and often boring. Isolated lighthouse locations, tedious work, and lack of human contact drove many a keeper to the brink of insanity. But once a keeper, always a keeper—and some believe many keepers maintained their duties from the beyond.

Nearly 250 lighthouses once perched along Michigan's 3,200 miles of Great Lakes shoreline. About half of Michigan's original lighthouses remain standing as a testament to the state's important maritime legacy.

Many a vessel passing strategic lighthouse-protected waters succumbed to wild Great Lakes storms. Vicious conditions took the lives of countless sailors. Situated at death's door, perhaps it's not surprising that an astonishing number of Michigan lighthouses are reportedly haunted.

The state's lighthouse chronicle began in 1825 before Michigan was granted statehood. Fort Gratiot Lighthouse along Lake

Huron was the first built. Almost all Michigan lighthouses existing today were constructed over the following fifty years, according to Central Michigan University's Clarke Historical Library documents. Lighthouses and keeper's quarters were constructed primarily of stone to withstand the battering from brutal spring and fall storms. The iconic conical tower design evolved to elevate lights for maximum visibility.

The keeper's life could be demanding and lonely, and offered only skimpy pay. Because the job was under federal jurisdiction, early keepers were political appointees. Married men between the ages of eighteen and fifty were the preferred candidates, as a keeper's wife and children could be counted on to share caretaking responsibilities. But it was an unending challenge for the government to maintain lighthouse staff. In his book *Great Lakes Lighthouse Tales*, Frederick Stonehouse notes that between 1885 and 1889, the government Lighthouse Board hired 1,190 new keepers. Of those, 680 resigned.

A keeper's primary duty was to maintain the station light from sunset to sunrise. By the 1870s, new hires were required to be able to read, write, and keep financial records. The keeper was a jack-of-all-trades, as duties required him to clean, paint, handle repairs, maintain equipment, and be able to sail and pull a boat.

When the day's work was done, keepers filled the empty hours with personal hobbies like rock collecting, reading, and building ship models. Many supplemented food supplies and boosted income by farming, fishing, and lumbering. Lake Superior's Manitou Island Lighthouse keeper Michael Fadden got himself into deep trouble with his chosen moonlighting activities. Fadden made bootleg whiskey on the side to sell to area Native Americans, but the arrangement eventually led to an ugly conflict with his customers. When federal authorities learned of the troubles, they fired Fadden and jailed him.

The last lighthouse was automated in 1983, forever ending the need for keepers to maintain the historic beacons. Until then, keepers were present when unfortunate disasters occurred and often performed and aided rescues. They sometimes housed and fed the rescued from their own meager resources. Such heroics were celebrated, but the dangers inherent in lighthouse work were perhaps underestimated. Keepers were stationed at Michigan lighthouses only during the navigation season, which began mid-March and ended in December, and they typically wintered in nearby towns. Traveling by small boats during the Great Lakes' most tumultuous months often proved a deadly challenge. In 1900 alone, five keepers died while making their way to their winter residences.

Michigan's lighthouse keepers were keenly aware of the importance of their job in guiding vessels through perilous waters. Some believe it's that dedication which locks their spirits to their stations, in some cases more than a century after their worldly departure. Lighthouse staff and visitors report supernatural presences carrying out keeper tasks, protecting people from threatening situations, and still standing guard from their lofty towers.

THE GHOST OF OLD PRESQUE ISLE LIGHTHOUSE

Despite being disconnected from power sources, the tower light at Old Presque Isle Lighthouse mysteriously continued to shine a light over Presque Isle Harbor. Some think it was the long-deceased care-taker's effort to ensure the lighthouse mission remained fulfilled.

Old Presque Isle Lighthouse, built in 1840, sits along a neck of land in the north arm of Presque Isle Bay between Rogers City and Alpena in northern Lake Huron. The sentinel marks the heart of an area known as Shipwreck Alley. In the early days of com-mercial sailing, Shipwreck Alley was considered one of the most treacherous routes in the Great Lakes system. At least two hundred vessels met their demise along this stretch, succumbing to turbulent storms, rocky shoals, collisions, fires, and ice.

Old Presque Isle Lighthouse, one of the oldest along the Great Lakes, supported safe passage into the harbor of refuge and refueling. The thirty-foot brick and stone tower originally pro-duced light by an array of eleven lamps fueled by whale oil. The lighthouse served thirty-one years before the federal government constructed a new Presque Isle Lighthouse one mile from the original to better serve as a coast light. The Old Lighthouse was decommissioned in 1871.

Old Presque Isle Lighthouse's classic conical structure and keeper's cottage sat abandoned for nearly three decades before being sold at public auction in 1897. It was bought and sold several times over until 1930, when Francis Stebbins purchased it from his uncle for use as a summer cottage. However, he found it unsuitable for his purpose. A lighthouse fan, he refurbished the tower in the 1950s to serve as a museum. Following his death, Francis's son, James, took possession of the historic lighthouse. In 1977, George and Lorraine Parris came on board as caretakers of the structures, both of which are listed on the Michigan and National Register of Historic Places.

The couple happily cared for the property and ran lighthouse tours for the next fifteen years. George developed a reputation with visitors as an entertaining tour guide. The couple loved their lighthouse life while it lasted. On a cold January day in 1992, George suddenly died. Like the wives of many lighthouse keepers before her, Lorraine carried on with the duties of operating the site.

A few months after George's passing, Lorraine was driving home from a social engagement when she spotted a light glowing in the lighthouse tower. She wondered how it was possible since George, with the aid of the Coast Guard, had disabled the light thirteen years earlier. She thought perhaps she was imagining it. Yet, every night after that, the tower's glow could be seen from points across the harbor. Lorraine became convinced it was George's way of keeping the spirit of the lighthouse alive.

Once word of the strange phenomenon reached the community, curious spectators came to see it for themselves. Local harbor masters were prompted to investigate the unexplained beam. They surmised that harbor dock lights reflected off the lantern room's glass panes. In a low-tech approach to solving the mystery, they shrouded the glass fronting the shore. The light disappeared, and they declared the mystery solved. Believers in the ghostly glow point out that the harbor masters only checked whether the light remained visible from across the harbor. Many still believed George continued his mission to preserve his beloved sentinel.

There were other persistent signs of George's presence, like the mornings Lorraine woke up smelling breakfast cooking when no one else was present. (George was known for taking pleasure in cooking breakfast.) Several guests described seeing a figure in the lantern room when it was unoccupied.

For Lorraine, the most convincing proof that George looked after the lighthouse from the beyond was the day he saved her life. Lorraine was exiting the lighthouse when a door appeared inexplicably jammed by chairs placed against it. As she tried to exit, a bolt of lightning struck near the lighthouse. Immediately after, the chairs slid away, allowing her to exit unharmed. Lorraine attributed her escape from harm to George's protection.

Presque Isle Township purchased the lighthouse in 1995 to preserve as a maritime cultural site. Visitors can decide for themselves whether George is responsible for friendly hauntings. The building and grounds are open to the public between mid-May and mid-October. There's a nominal fee to climb the circular stairs to the tower top where a priceless view of Presque Isle Harbor and the Lake Huron shoreline—and perhaps George—await.

The Haunting of Waugoshance

Not only was Waugoshance Lighthouse haunted by its keeper, but it was also bombed by the US military and repeatedly assaulted by Lake Michigan storms. While the government's official story is that Waugoshance Lighthouse was decommissioned because it was no longer needed, legend maintains no keeper could be found willing to work at the haunted sentinel.

Waugoshance was the first Great Lakes lighthouse constructed off the mainland entirely on a shoal. It sits at the northwest tip of the Mitten within Wilderness State Park jurisdiction seventeen miles west of the Mackinac Bridge. The lighthouse replaced the first lightship, which helped guide mariners through the Mackinac Straits for nearly twenty years. Through this passage came ships transporting lumber, coal, and goods to Lake Michigan ports, including Chicago. Other ships delivered grains and iron to Detroit and Cleveland. Because the lightship was expensive to maintain and its position was difficult to stabilize, Congress appropriated funds for the permanent station.

But constructing the offshore lighthouse's keeper quarters proved complicated, and it required five years to complete. In 1851, Waugoshance Lighthouse finally began operations, yet the work of maintaining the offshore station never ended. Lake Michigan's fierce battering continually threatened the structure, making ongoing repairs necessary.

The unique lighthouse with its seventy-six-foot tower housed what is believed to be the first Fresnel lens on the Great Lakes. The compact, powerful fourth-order Fresnel lens produced visibility of more than sixteen miles. Waugoshance Lighthouse was also distinguished by its birdcage-style lantern, one of only three remaining on the Great Lakes. Unlike typical lighthouse towers, Waugoshance's paint job featured red and white horizontal stripes.

Two ghosts are said to haunt Waugoshance. It's reported cries of a worker killed during construction have been heard at times. But the ghost of head keeper John Herman is said to be responsible for the most disruption.

Operating the Waugoshance station required a head keeper and two assistants. Herman was known for two things: He liked his liquor, and he enjoyed playing practical jokes. On an August night in 1894, Herman returned from shore leave drunk. It was his idea of fun to lock his assistant in the lantern room. The temporarily imprisoned assistant observed Herman stumble away, staggering along the pier. That was the last time anyone laid eyes on the living, breathing keeper. He was presumed drowned.

After Herman's death, unexplained things began to happen at the lighthouse. Doors opened and closed by themselves. The coal bin was mysteriously filled, although no one was around to accomplish the task. Anyone who fell asleep while on duty had the chair pulled out from under him. Word spread of the multitude of unexplained happenings at the lighthouse, and it became increasingly difficult for the government to hire keepers for Waugoshance. Despite luring potential keepers with pay higher than that offered at other lighthouses, no one wanted to live with Herman's ghost.

Waugoshance's history of hauntings and death earned it the nickname the "nautical gravestone." Because of difficulties at Waugoshance, the government decommissioned the station in 1912 after White Shoals Lighthouse, built just four miles away, became operational. After Waugoshance's shuttering, the hauntings reportedly ended.

But trouble for the decommissioned sentinel was not over. It was to become the focus of a new government secret. As World War II raged in the summer of 1943, the US Navy took possession of Waugoshance Point. Under the command of Naval Air Station Traverse City, the lighthouse became the target of a clandestine project engineered by Navy Special Task Air Group One. This early experimental drone program involved equipping twin-engine planes with radio-controlled steering mechanisms. The experimental drones dropped multiple bombs on Waugoshance. One landing near the lighthouse caused an explosion that set the station on fire, destroying its interior but leaving the exterior standing.

Following its role in drone development, the lighthouse was left to defend itself from Lake Michigan's fury. In 1983, the enduring structure was listed on the National Register of Historic Places. In 2011, the US Coast Guard granted ownership to the Waugoshance Lighthouse Preservation Society for restoration purposes.

Because the lighthouse is only viewable by boat, Mackinaw City boat operators provide lighthouse cruises for viewing Waugoshance and other Mackinac Straits light stations.

SEUL CHOIX'S PHANTOM KEEPER

The determined spirit of a Seul Choix Pointe Lighthouse keeper regularly appears at the historic sentinel, which some claim is the most haunted lighthouse on the Great Lakes.

The lighthouse sits along the northernmost shores of Lake Michigan, fourteen miles east of the Upper Peninsula town of Manistique. Seul Choix was named by French sailors who considered the site the "only choice" for refuge from storms. Not all sailors found escape from Mother Nature's fury, however. More than twenty-four shipwrecks occurred in the waters near the station, and as many as five hundred are said to have lost their lives within the beacon's glow.

In the late 1880s, these treacherous waters were vital to ships supporting Escanaba's growing iron-ore trade. In 1886, Congress approved funds for the lighthouse complex, but due to a series of delays, the structure didn't become a reality until the summer of 1895. Seul Choix's nearly seventy-nine-foot brick tower housed a third-order Fresnel lens until the lighthouse was automated by the US Coast Guard in 1972. The following year, its care was abandoned.

Five keepers maintained Seul Choix throughout its service life. One refused to leave: Captain Joseph Willie Townshend, the second keeper. Townshend and his third wife, Ruth, moved into Seul Choix in 1901. He was a bearded, cigar-smoking character who in 1910 succumbed to a sudden and painful death in an upstairs bedroom of the keeper's quarters. Following his passing, people began to report a ghostly image appearing in a mirror in the same room. The bushy beard, moustache, and eyebrows were unmistakably that of Townshend. Bolts of electricity have also been known to shoot from the mirror.

Since the keeper's death, many spooky, but innocent, paranormal occurrences have been reported, including the unexplained scent of cigar smoke and the sound of mysterious footsteps. Chairs move and kitchen utensils are rearranged with forks set tines down, just as the keeper preferred. The president of the Gulliver Historical Society, Marilyn Fischer, reports paranormal experts claim Townshend is kept company by his wife's spirit and three other ghosts. Communicating through a medium, Townshend told Fischer he intends to remain faithful to his Seul Choix Lighthouse duties.

In 1977, the Michigan Department of Natural Resources purchased the Seul Choix Point property for use as a park. While owned by the state, Seul Choix Point Lighthouse Park and Museums are today operated by the Gulliver Historical Society. As many as twenty-two thousand people visit annually to explore the restored keeper's house and assistant keeper's house, enjoy tower tours, and visit the Fog Signal Area History Museum, Boat House Museum, Oil House Museum, gift shop, thirty-seat theater, and Research/Genealogy Library.

MEET THE SPIRIT OF THE GRAND TRAVERSE LIGHTHOUSE

At the tip of Leelanau Peninsula—where fog rolls in like a ghostly blanket spread over the rocky Lake Michigan shoreline—the spirit of an old-time keeper roams. You can help the ghost of keeper Captain Peter Nelson maintain Grand Traverse Lighthouse through its volunteer keeper program. Stay in the assistant keeper's quarters, man the museum, and listen for the eerie footsteps of the long-deceased Nelson.

Grand Traverse Lighthouse dates to 1852 and is listed on the Michigan and National Register of Historic Places. It guards the entrance to Grand Traverse Bay and the Manitou Passage. In its service heyday, it aided schooners carrying grains, meats, whiskey, and other goods. The original station was relocated to its present site and rebuilt in 1858 as a two-and-a-half story brick house featuring a rooftop tower.

Nelson served as keeper at the second location from 1874 to 1890. He died two years after his earthly departure from lighthouse service, but some believe he remains on duty. Staff and visitors report hearing footsteps climb the tower stairs when no one is present. They experience a paranormal presence brush past them and hear voices coming out of thin air. It's suspected that Captain Nelson's spirit may keep company with the apparitions of three other individuals known to have died at the lighthouse.

STEFANI STALEY

Volunteer keepers join the ghost of Captain Peter Nelson at Grand Traverse Lighthouse.

In 1932, the US Coast Guard converted the site at Northport with its lighthouse and buildings into Leelanau State Park. The lighthouse was restored to replicate what it looked like in the 1920s and 1930s. State park visitors may tour the structure and grounds and attempt to commiserate with the keeper who refuses to leave his post.

THE MOURNING KEEPER OF POINTE AUX BARQUES

The ghost of the Great Lakes' first woman lighthouse keeper is said to lurk in the upper rooms of the Pointe aux Barques keeper's house. The original lighthouse was built in 1848 along Lake Huron at the tip of Michigan's thumb near Port Hope. Lighthouse property is surrounded by the Thumb Bottomland Preserve, where nearly twenty ships met their demise. The remote lighthouse site carved out of coastal wilderness was highly vulnerable to Lake Huron's harsh weather. Violent storms took a toll on the lighthouse, and fire damaged the keeper's cottage. In 1857, a new cottage and eighty-nine-foot tower were constructed.

Beginning his tenure in 1848, Peter Shook was the first Pointe aux Barques keeper. Only one year later, his boat capsized while sailing to Port Huron for supplies. Shook and his three companions perished, like many others involved in early maritime work. And like many spouses, Shook's wife, Catherine, was left with the important duty of maintaining the station. Because of her unfortunate circumstance, she made her mark on history as the inland seas' first female keeper.

Some say not even death caused Catherine Shook to abandon her lighthouse. Visitors report seeing the spirit of a mourning woman walk the grounds, and an apparition reportedly appears in a second-floor window. Some report hearing strange voices, hearing footsteps on the tower stairs, and feeling an unexplained cold chill.

In 2010, representatives of the Southeast Michigan Paranormal Society paid the lighthouse a visit to investigate the spooky happenings. They reported hearing the same phenomena as were rumored and concluded the lighthouse is indeed haunted.

The restored Pointe aux Barques Lighthouse is the cornerstone of Huron County's Lighthouse Park and Museum. The lighthouse, which was in use for more than 150 years, is open to the public from Memorial Day to mid-October. Lighthouse Park spans 120 acres and contains 110 campsites for those brave enough to face off with the lighthouse ghost in the dark of night.

BIBLIOGRAPHY

CHAPTER 1: DELTA COUNTY'S TREASURE ISLAND

Bennett, Richard. www.bennettvideo.com.

Keefe, William. "Legends Still Hint of Gold Near Poverty Island." *The Beacher,* July 19, 2001.

———. "The Roster of Goldseekers Reaches to Poverty Island." *The Beacher,* September 27, 2001.

LaSalle-Griffon Project. www.lasalle-griffon.com.

Lundstrom, Jim. "The Search for La Salle's Lost Ship 'Le Griffon' Continues." *Door County Pulse,* February 9, 2018.

Stonehouse, Frederick. *Great Lakes Lighthouse Tales.* Gwinn, MI: Avery Color Studios, 1998.

Sullivan, Patrick. "Poverty Island in Lake Michigan." *Traverse City Record-Eagle,* August 16, 2007.

Walsh-Sarnecki, Peggy. "Mystery of the *Griffon:* Search for Great Lakes Oldest Shipwreck." *Detroit Free Press,* January 2, 2006.

White, Ed. "The Griffin? Deal Struck to Determine Shipwreck ID." Associated Press, August 13, 2010.

CHAPTER 2: THE MYSTERIOUS DISAPPEARANCE OF JIMMY HOFFA

Ashman, Charles, and Rebecca Sobel. *The Strange Disappearance of Jimmy Hoffa.* New York: Manor Books, 1976.

Associated Press. "FBI Searches Michigan Horse Farm for Hoffa's Remains." May 19, 2006.

Bland, Eric. "Cadaver-Sniffing Device Could Find Jimmy Hoffa." NBC News, August 13, 2010. www.news.discovery.com.

Bradley, Tahman. "Is Detroit Dig Latest Search for Jimmy Hoffa's Body?" ABC News, September 5, 2019. www.abcnews.go.com.

Brandt, Charles. *I Heard You Paint Houses.* Hanover, NH: Steerforth Press, 2004.

Hansen, Jeffry Scott. *Digging for the Truth: The Final Resting Place of Jimmy Hoffa.* Detroit, MI: Spectre Publishing, 2009.

Horowitz, Carl. "Transcripts Show Jimmy Hoffa Loyalists Plotted to Kill FBI Agents." National Legal and Policy Center, August 11, 2009. www.nlpc.org.

Krouse, Peter. "Testimony of Key Witness in Jimmy Hoffa Case Unsealed." Cleveland.com, April 15, 2009. www.cleveland.com.

Mafia International. www.realdealmafia.com/mobcorner_hoffa.html.

Martinez, Edecio. "What Jimmy Hoffa Knew: Did Powerful Teamsters Boss Plot to Ambush FBI?" CBS News, July 27, 2009. www.cbsnews.com.

Time. "Labor: Jimmy Hoffa's Disappearance." August 11, 1975. www.time.com.

USA Today. "Alas, No Jimmy Hoffa as Giants Stadium Tumbles Down." April 1, 2010. www.content.usatoday.com.

Zacharias, Pat. "The Day Jimmy Hoffa Didn't Come Home." *Detroit News,* August 28, 1999.

CHAPTER 3: MICHIGAN'S MINI STONEHENGE

"Beaver Island History from the Beaver Island Historical Society." BeaverIsland.net. www.beaverisland.net/History.

Eschborn, Archie. "The Great Beaver Island Stone Circle and Map Stone." In *The Best of Astrea.* Bloomington, IN: AuthorHouse, 2006.

Flesher, John. "Mastodon? Rock Brings History to Surface." *Traverse City Record-Eagle,* September 5, 2007.

Janega, James. "Underwater Stones Puzzle Archeologists." *Chicago Tribune,* February 8, 2009.

Joseph, Frank, ed. *Discovering the Mysteries of Ancient America: Lost History and Legends, Unearthed and Explored.* Franklin Lakes, NJ: New Page Books, 2006.

Sodders, Betty. "Questionable Rocks with a Prehistory Past, Part I, Beaver Island." In *Michigan Prehistory Mysteries.* Marquette, MI: Avery, 1990.

CHAPTER 4: THE DEADLY GREAT LAKES TRIANGLE

A&E Television Network. *Deep Sea Detectives: Death of the Edmund Fitzgerald.* July 22, 2003.

Alan Landsburg Productions. *In Search of . . . The Great Lakes Triangle.* November 2, 1978.

Gittleman, Linda. "Passengers Left Note in Dr. Hall's Medical Bag." *Morning Sun,* July 25, 2010. www.themorningsun.com/articles/2010/07/24/news/doc4c4b78faa4eb1588880903.

Gourley, Jay. *The Great Lakes Triangle.* Greenwich, CT: Fawcett Publications, 1977.

Great Lakes Monitoring. "The Fate of the Christmas Tree Ship." www.epa.gov/glnpo/monitoring/great_minds_great_lakes/history/christmas_tree.html.

———. "Shipwrecks." www.epa.gov/glnpo/monitoring/great_minds_great_lakes/history/shipwrecks.html.

Great Lakes Shipwreck Museum. "Television Program Focuses upon the History and Quality of Shipwreck Museum, Society, and Whitefish Point." www.shipwreckmuseum.com/press-releases-49.

Heath, Gord. "Missing F-89 Found?" UFO*BC. www.ufobc.ca/kinross/greatLakesDiveCo/greatLakesDiveCoMain.htm.

Keyhoe, Donald. *Aliens from Space.* New York: Signet, 1979.

Korgen, Ben. "Bonanza for Lake Superior: Seiches Do More than Move Water." Minnesota Sea Grant. www.seagrant.umn.edu/

newsletter/2000/02/bonanza_for_lake_superior_seiches_do_more_than_move_water.html.

Longacre, Glen. "The Christmas Tree Ship: Captain Herman E. Schuenemann and the Schooner *Rouse Simmons*." The National Archives. www.archives.gov/publications/prologue/2006/winter/christmas-tree.html.

Michigan State University. "Seiches on the Great Lakes." www.geo.msu.edu/geogmich/seiches.htm.

National Investigations Committee on Aerial Phenomena. "The Kinross Incident." www.nicap.org/reports/kinross3.htm.

National Transportation Safety Board. Preliminary Aviation Report CEN10FA465. www.ntsb.gov/ntsb/GenPDF.asp?id=CEN10FA465&rpt=p.

Stonehouse, Frederick. *The Wreck of the Edmund Fitzgerald*. Marquette, MI: Lake Superior Press, 1996.

Van Heest, Valerie. "Remembering Northwest Flight 2501." www.northwestflight2501.org/NorthwestFlight2501.

CHAPTER 5: PAUL BUNYAN: FOLKLORE OR FAKELORE?

Beck, E. C. *They Knew Paul Bunyan*. Ann Arbor: University of Michigan Press, 1956.

Dorson, Richard M. Papers, 1940–1980, bulk 1962–1977. Indiana University Office of University Archives and Records Management. www.msu.edu/user/singere/fakelore.html.

Fitzmaurice, John. *The Shanty Boy*. Berrien Springs, MI: Hardscrabble Books, 1979.

Houston, Kay, "The Man Who Could Out-Lumber Paul Bunyan." *Detroit News,* June 14, 1996.

Michigan House Democrats. "Michigan House Declares Oscoda Home of Paul Bunyan." http://103.housedems.com/news/article/michigan-house-declares-oscoda-home-of-paul-bunyan/sheltrown-sees-quick-acceptance-of-house-resolution-141.

Rogers, Laurence. *Paul Bunyan: How a Terrible Timber Feller Became a Legend*. Bay City, MI: Historical Press, 1933.

Sandburg, Carl. *Harvest Poems: 1910–1960*. New York: Harcourt, Brace, Jovanovich, 1960.

Singer, Eliot. "Fakelore, Multiculturalism and the Ethics of Children's Literature." www.msu.edu/user/singere/fakelore.html.

CHAPTER 6: THE GHOST LIGHTS OF PAULDING AND EVART

Blakeslee, Sandra. "Earthquake Lights Linked to Bubbles." *New York Times,* December 10, 1991. www.nytimes.com/1991/12/10/science/science-watch-earthquake-lights-linked-to-bubbles.html.

Dacey, James. "A Radon Detector for Earthquake Prediction." http://physicsworld.com/cws/article/news/42015.

Godfrey, Linda. *Weird Michigan: Your Travel Guide to Michigan's Local Legends and Best Kept Secrets*. New York: Sterling, 2006.

Goodrich, Marcia. "Michigan Tech Students Solve the Mystery of the Paulding Light." *Michigan Tech News,* October 28, 2010.

Hunter, Gerald. *More Haunted Michigan: New Encounters with Ghosts of the Great Lakes State.* Holt, MI: Thunder Bay Press, 2006.

Hunts' Guide to Michigan's Upper Peninsula. "Paulding Mystery Light." http://hunts-upguide.com/paulding.html.

United States Geological Survey. "Radon Potential of the Upper Midwest." http://energy.cr.usgs.gov/radon/midwest4.html.

WWTV/WWUP–TV. "Glowing Evart Tombstones." www .9and10news.com/Category/Story/?cID=31&id=267699.

CHAPTER 7: WHO WAS THE ORIGINAL ROSIE THE RIVETER?

Ahern, Louise. "Lansing Woman Was Model for Iconic Image." *Lansing State Journal,* December 30, 2010.

Colman, Penny. *Rosie the Riveter: Women Working on the Home Front in World War II.* New York: Crown Publishers, 1995.

Ford Motor Company. "The Real Story of Rosie the Riveter: A Ford Motor Company Employee." http://corporate.ford.com/ about-ford/heritage/people/rosietheriveter/657-rosie-the -riveter.

Fox, Margalit. "Naomi Parker Fraley, the Real Rosie the Riveter, Dies at 96." *New York Times,* January 22, 2018.

Frank, Miriam, Marilyn Ziebarth, and Connie Field. *The Life and Times of Rosie the Riveter*. Emeryville, CA: Clarity Educational Productions, 1982.

Garrett, Nicole. "World War II Arsenal." Michigan Department of Natural Resources and Environment. www.michigan.gov/dnr/0,1607,7-153-54463_19313_20652_19271_19357-152471--,00.html.

Marcano, Tony. "Famed Riveter in War Effort, Rose Monroe Dies at 77." *New York Times*, June 2, 1997.

National Park Service. "Rosie the Riveter: Women Working During World War II." www.nps.gov/pwro/collection/website/rosie.htm.

Rosie the Riveter World War II Home Front Historic National Park. "Rockwell's Rosie the Riveter Rockwell Painting Auctioned." www.rosietheriveter.org/painting.htm.

Shapiro, Rees. "Geraldine Doyle; Inspired Rosie the Riveter Poster." *Washington Post,* December 31, 2010.

CHAPTER 8: EXTRATERRESTRIAL VISITORS

Baulch, Vivian. "The Great Michigan UFO Chase." *Detroit News,* February 14, 1995.

Cameron, Grant. "Gerald Ford UFOs." Center for UFO Studies, August 1, 2009. www.cufos.org/org.html.

Carter, Brody. "UFO's in West Michigan? Maybe." Fox 17 West Michigan, February 7, 1018.

Cox, Billy. "Getting the UFO Story Told." *Herald Tribune,* June 18, 2007.

Dossier UFO. "Condon Committee." http://dossierufo.com/ index.php?option=com_content&view=article&id=41: ccc&catid=2:articles&Itemid=3.

Ford Congressional Papers. "Radio Broadcast Regarding Michigan UFO Sightings." March 25, 1966.

Ford, Congressman Gerald. News Release Regarding 1966 Michigan UFO Sightings. UFO Folder 1966, Press Secretary & Speech File 1947–1973 Box 9D.

———. Radio Broadcast Regarding 1966 Michigan UFO Sightings, Radio Tape for Fifth District Stations March 30, 1966. Jerry Ford Papers, Press Secretary & Speech Files 1948– 1973, Weekly Radio Reports Box D35.

———. Statement by House Minority Leader Gerald R. Ford, R-Michigan, April 21, 1966. Jerry Ford Papers, 1947–1973, Folder UFOs 1966, Press & Secretary Speech File Box D9.

———. Statement by House Minority Leader Gerald R. Ford. Jerry Ford Papers, 1947–1973, Folder UFOs 1966, Press & Secretary Speech File Box D9.

Independent Crop Circle Researchers' Association. ICCRA Crop Circle Research Reports for the State of Michigan. www.iccra .org/reports.htm.

Marsh, Roger. "Michigan Witness Reports UFO." *The Canadian,* February 3, 2011.

Michigan Mutual UFO Network. www.mufon.com.

Palmer, Ken. "Crop of Circles Baffles." *Flint Sun Journal,* October 21, 2007.

Shepherd, John. "Earth Station One." Project STRAT. www .projectstrat.com.

United States Air Force. "Unidentified Flying Objects and Air Force Project Blue Book." www.af.mil/information/factsheets/ factsheet_print.asp?fsID=188&page=1.

Walsh, Michael. "Interest Soars in Recent UFO Sighting Over Lake." *Grand Rapids Press Service,* March 13, 1994.

WorldNetDaily. "Michigan Crop Circles 'No Hoax.'" August 6, 2003. www.wnd.com/?pageId=20135.

CHAPTER 9: THE UNDERGROUND RAILROAD'S SECRET QUILT CODE

Cohen, Noam. "In Frederick Douglass Tribute, Slave Folklore and Fact Collide." *New York Times,* January 23, 2007.

Dobard, Raymond, PhD, and Jacqueline Tobin. *Hidden in Plain View.* New York: Anchor Books, 2000.

Fellner, Leigh. "From Meme to Monument: How the Underground Quilt Code Ended Up on a Statue of Frederick Douglass." www.fabrics.net/joan507.asp.

Ives, Sarah. "Did Quilts Hold Codes to the Underground Railroad?" *National Geographic,* February 5, 2004.

Larson, Clifford Kate. "Who Used and How Were Quilts Used?" Underground Railroad Research Forum. www.afrigeneas.com/forum-ugrr/index.cgi/md/read/id/278.

Mull, Carol. *The Underground Railroad in Michigan.* Jefferson, NC: McFarland & Company, 2010.

State of Michigan. "Slavery, Resistance and the Underground Railroad in Michigan." www.michigan.gov/dnr/0,1607,7-153 -54463_18670_44390-158647--,00.html.

Stukin, Stacie. "Unraveling the Myth of Quilts and the Underground Railroad." *Time, April 3, 2007.* www.time.com/time/arts/article/0,8599,1606271,00.html.

Wulfert, Kimberly, PhD. "Quilts and the Underground Railroad Revisited: Interview with Historian Giles R. Wright." www .antiquequiltdating.com/Quilts_and_the_Underground_ Railroad_Revisited_-_Interview_with_Historian_Giles_R._ Wright.html.

CHAPTER 10: LORDS OF THE UNDERWORLD

Albion Downtown Development Authority. "Historic Albion Purple Gang Walking Tour." http://www.albiondda.org/files/Purple_Gang_Brochure.pdf.

Burnstein, Scott. *Motor City Mafia: A Century of Organized Crime in Detroit.* Charleston, SC: Arcadia Publishing, 2006.

Field, Susan. "Home Linked to Purple Gang Has Long History." *Morning Sun,* January 30, 2011.

———. "Purple Gang's History in Clare Still Remembered." *Oakland Press,* January 17, 2011.

Kavieff, Paul. *Detroit's Infamous Purple Gang.* Charleston, SC: Arcadia Publishing, 2008.

———. "Detroit's Infamous Purple Gang." *Detroit News,* July 16, 1999.

Nolan, Jenny. "How Prohibition Made Detroit a Bootlegger's Dream Town." *Detroit News,* June 15, 1999.

Simpson-Mersha, Isis. "Purple Gang Attorney's Home Featured in Clare Gardening Tour." *Saginaw News,* July 12, 2017. https://www.mlive.com/news/saginaw/index.ssf/2017/07/former_attorney_to_gangsters_h.html.

Walkerville Times. "Mobsters, Mayhem & Murder." www.walkervilletimes.com/34/mobsters1.html.

Whitall, Susan. "The Purple Gang's Bloody Legacy." *Detroit News,* June 9, 2001.

CHAPTER 11: THE BURIED CITY OF SINGAPORE

Dunbar, Willis, and George May. *Michigan, a History of the Wolverine State.* Grand Rapids, MI: Wm. B. Eerdmans Publishing Co., 1988.

Lane, Kit. *Buried Singapore: Michigan's Imaginary Pompeii.* Douglas, MI: Pavilion Press, 1994.

Lane, Kit, and Robert Simonds. *Lost & Found: Ghost Towns of the Saugatuck Area.* Douglas, MI: Saugatuck Historical Society, 2000.

Massie, Larry. *Copper Trails & Iron Rails.* Allegan Forest, MI: Priscilla Press, 1999.

National Park Service. "Sleeping Bear Dunes 'Ghost Towns.'" www.nps.gov/slbe/historyculture/ghosttowns.htm.

CHAPTER 12: LEGENDS OF THE FOREST

Bigfoot Field Researchers Organization. "About the Bigfoot Field Researchers Organization." www.bfro.net/REF/aboutbfr.asp.

———. "Michigan Sightings." www.bfro.net/GDB/state_listing .asp?state=mi.

———. Report #26782 (Class A). www.bfro.net/GDB/state_ listing.asp?state=mi.

———. "What Are the Undisputed Facts about the Bigfoot/ Sasquatch Mystery?" www.bfro.net.

Brissette, Elon. "Local Resident Researching Bigfoot Phenomena." *Ogemaw County Herald,* July 23, 2009.

Cohen, Amy. "A Bigfoot in the Thumb?" *Detroit News,* November 22, 1981.

Cook, Eric. "A Kalamazoo Native's Story Helps to Debunk the Myth of Bigfoot Tomorrow on TV Land." *Kalamazoo Gazette,* November 18, 2008.

Garland Swamp Dogman. www.northernexpress.com/news/ feature/article-3386-call-of-the-wild-dogman/

Legend of Michigan's Dogman. www.absolutemichigan.com/ michigan/the-legend-of-the-michigan-dogman/

Lovgren, Stefan. "Forensic Expert Says Bigfoot Is Real." *National Geographic,* October 23, 2003.

Payne, Amy. "Despite Skeptics, West Branch Bigfoot Devotee Making Presentations about Sightings." *Booth Mid-Michigan,* February 27, 2009.

Singer, Marci. "Bigfoot: Legend or . . ." *Petoskey News,* October 30, 2009.

Taylor, Jodee. "Dogman Legend Gets Hollywood Treatment." *Traverse City Record Eagle,* March 19, 2010.

Weird Michigan. "Monsters." www.weirdmichigan.com/monsters .html.

Westrum, Ron, PhD. "Sasquatch & Scientists: Reporting Scientific Anomalies." www.bigfootencounters.com/biology/ scientists.htm.

CHAPTER 13: THE TRUTH BEHIND MICHIGAN'S MUSES

"Constantino Brumidi." Architect of the Capitol. www.aoc.gov/ capitol-hill/artists/constantino-brumidi.

Dutchas, Geoffrey G. "Artist on Loan: Tommaso Juglaris and the Italian Immigrant Experience in America's Late Gilded Age."

https://qcpages.qc.cuny.edu/calandra/sites/calandra.i-italy.org/
files/files/Drutchas%20from%20IAR-1_1-Text-4.pdf.

"Haymarket Riot." History.com, updated October 9, 2019. www
.history.com/topics/haymarket-riot.

Hayward, Peter. "Visions of Heaven." *Tufts University Tufts
Journal*, November 29, 2010.

"Italian-American Organizations of Metro Detroit Celebrate
the 'Year of Italian Culture in the United States 2013' with
Tommaso Juglaris Exhibition." We the Italians, September 30,
2013. www.wetheitalians.com/art-heritage-great-lakes/italian
-american-organizations-of-metro-detroit-celberate-the-year
-of-italian-culture-in-the-united-states-2013-with-tommaso
-juglaris-exhibition.

Juglaris, Tommaso, and Maria Luisa Reviglio della Veneria.
Tommaso Juglaris: An Artist Between Europe and America.
Moncalieri, Italy: Famija Moncalerisa, 2004.

Lansing Newspapers in Education, Inc., and the Michigan
Historical Center. "The Mystery of the Muses." *Michigan Time
Traveler*. www.michigan.gov/documents/hal_mhc_mhm_
muses_10-13-2004_105772_7.pdf.

Lichtenstein, Nelson, et al. "Nativism and Immigration
Restriction." In *Who Built America: Working People and the
Nation's Economy, Politics, Culture and Society,* vol. 2, 2nd ed.
Boston and New York: Bedford/St. Martin's, 2000.

Michigan Capitol Commission. *Michigan State Capitol Art Guide*. http://capitol.michigan.gov/ArtGuide.

Michigan Legislature. *Your State Capitol*. www.legislature.mi.gov/documents/publications/YourStateCapitol.pdf.

Michigan State Capitol. "Plan a Tour." http://capitol.michigan .gov/plantour.

"Painting Michigan's Muses." Through an Artist's Eyes: Tommaso Jugaris in Europe and America. www.juglaris.org/25-painting.

"Michigan's Capitol Muses." Through an Artist's Eyes: Tommaso Juglaris in Europe and America. www.juglaris.org/47 -michigans.

"Michigan's Capitol Mystery." Through an Artist's Eyes: Tommaso Jugaris in Europe and America. www.juglaris.org/53-michigans.

United States Department of the Interior. National Historic Landmarks Nomination: Michigan State Capitol. https:// npgallery.nps.gov/pdfhost/docs/NHLS/Text/71000396.pdf.

CHAPTER 14: LIGHTHOUSE KEEPERS FROM THE BEYOND

"About Thunder Bay National Marine Sanctuary." National Marine Sanctuaries, National Oceanic & Atmospheric Administration. https://thunderbay.noaa.gov/about/welcome .html.

Beeler, Jennifer, Steve Millburg, and Mamie Walling. "Seul Choix Lighthouse, Gulliver, Michigan." *Coastal Living*, August 24,

2011. www.coastalliving.com/travel/top-15-haunted
-lighthouses#haunted-lighthouses-seul-choix-point-lighthouse.

Carter, Elliot. "Ruins of the Waugoshance Light Station." Atlas
Obscura. www.atlasobscura.com/places/ruins-waugoshance
-lighthouse.

Edwards, Jack. "A Nautical Gravestone." *Lighthouse Digest*,
September 1998. www.lighthousedigest.com/Digest/StoryPage
.cfm?StoryKey=368.

"Ghost at the Grand Traverse Lighthouse." Leelanau.com,
October 30, 2008. http://leelanau.com/ghost-at-the-grand
-traverse-lighthouse.

"History of Michigan Lighthouses." Central Michigan University
Clarke Historical Library. www.cmich.edu/library/clarke/
ResearchResources/Michigan_Material_Statewide/Michigan
_Lighthouses/Pages/History-of-Michigan-Lighthouses.aspx.

Langley, Jan. "The question Is: 'Is Pointe aux Barques Haunted?'"
Huron County View, May 5, 2010.

"A Light Mystery." *Lighthouse Digest*, October 1998. www
.lighthousedigest.com/Digest/StoryPage.cfm?StoryKey=369.

"Old Presque Isle Lighthouse (1840)." Presque Isle Township
Museum Society. http://presqueislelighthouses.org/
lighthouses/old-presque-isle-lighthouse-1840.

Pendowski, Shelby. "Grand Traverse Lighthouse a Beacon of
Hope since 1852." *Leelanau Enterprise,* July 10, 2014.

"Pointe Aux Barques Lighthouse." Lighthousefriends.com. http://lighthousefriends.com/light.asp?ID=171.

Pointe Aux Barques Lighthouse Society. www.pointeauxbarques lighthouse.org.

"Presque Isle (Old) Lighthouse." Lighthousefriends.com. http://lighthousefriends.com/light.asp?ID=180.

Robinson, John. "Haunted Michigan: The Apparition of Pointe Aux Barques Lighthouse." 99.1 WFMK, September 14, 2016.

"Seul Choix Point Lighthouse." Lighthousefriends.com. http://lighthousefriends.com/light.asp?ID=565.

"Seul Choix Pointe Lighthouse." Pure Michigan. www.michigan .org/property/seul-choix-pointe-lighthouse.

"Seul Choix Point Lighthouse on Lake Michigan: The Haunted Lighthouse." Exploring the North. www.exploringthenorth .com/seulchoix/seul.html.

Sonnenberg, Mike. "Ten Haunted or Creepy Places in Michigan." Lost in Michigan, October 16, 2014. http://lostinmichigan .net/haunted-creepy-places-michigan.

Stonehouse, Frederick. *Great Lakes Lighthouse Tales*. Gwinn, MI: Avery Color Studios, 1998.

"Waugoshance Lighthouse." Lighthousefriends.com. http://lighthousefriends.com/light.asp?ID=211.

Wright, Larry, and Patricia Wright. *Great Lakes Lighthouses Encyclopedia*. Erin, ON: Boston Mills Press, 2011.

INDEX

About The Author

Sally Barber has dedicated her writing career to celebrating Michigan's people, places, and events. She is co-author of the regional bestseller, *The Insiders' Guide to Michigan's Traverse Bay Region* and author of *The Michigan Eco-Traveler*. She has penned community publications for more than thirty of the state's cities. Sally is a frequent contributor to Michigan's major newspapers and its business magazines. The writer lives within the heart of the Manistee National Forest among its towering pines and where deer, eagles, and bears are among her neighbors.